DORSE INDUSTRIAL I

Peter Stanier

Lano's Arch, Tout Quarry.

INTRODUCTION

THE COUNTY of Dorset summons up a vision far removed from 'industry': an idyllic rural landscape, with chalk downs, wooded vales, water-meadows and picturesque villages – an image much enhanced by the writings of Thomas Hardy who wrote just at the time when industry and in particular the railway age were beginning to affect Dorset life. The Dorset landscape was almost unscathed by 'progress', although tourism along some parts of the coast and the great urban sprawl of Bournemouth-Poole (much formerly inside Hampshire until 1974), and perhaps Weymouth, are the exception to the rule. It is true that Dorset was undisturbed by heavy industry, yet it offers evidence for a surprising variety of industrial activities, almost all based on natural resources, from geology or products of the land. The major industries have been agriculture, the working of stone and clay, rope and net making, brewing and milling.

Industrial archaeology is concerned with the material relics of man's past activities, especially in the nineteenth century, but beginning in the mid-eighteenth century – the period of the Industrial Revolution. Some industries, such as milling or quarrying, have a longer history and were already well established in the Middle Ages.

Dorset has a long industrial history. The Isle of Purbeck was the centre of industry in the Iron Age through into the Roman period. Armlets of Kimmeridge shale were turned on pole lathes at settlement sites. The discarded cores are known as Kimmeridge Coal Money. In the Roman period there was large scale production at Rope Lake Hole, east of Kimmeridge, while at Norden more fancy goods were made such as table legs, platters and tesserae. Norden was also a production centre for Purbeck marble, where it was made into monuments, decorative furniture inlays, mortars and tesserae. Pottery was produced on a commercial scale from the first century AD, using the clays around Poole Harbour, while salt was produced in clay vats along the south side of Poole Harbour and at Kimmeridge. There are finds in various local museums, but especially the County Museum in Dorchester. Of Roman roads in Dorset, the Ackling Dyke across Oakley Down near Sixpenny Handley is one of the best preserved sections in the whole country. There was an aqueduct supplying water to Roman Dorchester (Durnovaria), and much of its length can be traced as an earthwork on the south side of the Frome valley.

The extractive industries were important in Dorset. The Purbeck marble industry was revived in medieval times, when this shelly limestone (not a true marble) was in demand for decorative work in churches. Portland stone is world famous, best known for its use in Wren's St Paul's Cathedral and many London landmarks. It could be sent easily by sea and was in demand long before Wren, and its quarries are still at work. There was limestone quarrying elsewhere, notably around Purbeck (underground here), Bridport, Marnhull and Sherborne. Limestone and chalk were quarried to burn in limekilns, another typically rural industry. Greensand was quarried along the escarpments near Shaftesbury, and another source of building stone came from the sandy heath stones of south-east Dorset.

Increasing demand for high quality Purbeck ball clay, exported for pottery making, fostered one of the earliest tramways in southern England in 1806. The clay is still worked in open pits and mines. Dorset had its own clay based potteries and tile works. Of these, the Verwood potteries produced earthenwares of great charac-

Clay sheds of Pike Bros., Fayle & Co., Corfe Castle.

ter. Other clays have been worked for brick making throughout Dorset, with the greatest concentration around Poole. Cement was made at Lyme Regis and Wareham. The latter was set up at Ridge in the 1870s by Thomas Powell, and used chalk marl quarried at Cocknowle.

Other minerals which have been worked were ironstone, gypsum, alum, copperas and oil shale. There being no coal to power the Industrial Revolution in Dorset, this last has been worked for its fuel content, especially at Kimmeridge where it was once used to fire a glassworks. Kimmeridge was also the site of salt pans, as were Lyme Regis, Charmouth and the shores of Poole Harbour. This was once a profitable business, and salt was exported to France in the fifteenth century.

Dorset's streams and rivers have provided power for many corn mills, in the form of waterwheels and, later, turbines. Water power was also applied to breweries, foundries, flax mills, saw mills, silk mills and paper mills. Paper making also required a clear stream of water. Flax and then rags and ropes were used for the fibre. There were paper mills at Beaminster, Wareham and Wimborne. The last was first mentioned in 1739, and from here Stephen Burt moved upstream to Witchampton in 1790. Burt's paper mill has been the only one in Dorset since 1832, although it has undergone much change in layout and ownership. It is still in operation.

The net and rope industry around Bridport was in demand by the navy and shipping industry for centuries. It was originally based on flax grown on the hillsides, and hemp grown in the fertile valley bottoms. The Bridport hemp was said to be the finest in Europe, but much was later imported. Flax was used for making sailcloth and linen.

Dorset's beer has been famous and its breweries are among the best industrial monuments in the county. Indeed, until the closure of the Devenish brewery at Weymouth in the 1980s, there were four independent brewers still in operation.

Turnpike roads and railways have been well documented, but there were no canals in Dorset. Nothing came of one suggested along the Frome valley from Wareham which would have given Dorchester access to Poole Harbour. The ambitious Dorset & Somerset Canal was authorised in 1796, but only parts in Somerset were built. It was intended to enter north Dorset, crossing the Blackmore Vale to join a canalised River Stour at Gain's Cross, and thence to the Poole area. The promoters were so confident that its course appears on Thomas Dix's *New Map of the County of Dorset*, published in 1820. Had it been built, coal from the Somerset coalfield could have been brought cheaply into south Dorset, a task later performed by the Somerset & Dorset Railway which followed a similar route.

Today, some apparently sleepy rural villages hide a much more industrious past. Bourton in north Dorset is a fine example of an industrial village a hundred years ago. The parish population was just 838 in 1881, and it is worth quoting from a directory of the time:

"Here are an iron foundry and boiler and agricultural implement manufactory of some celebrity and extent, two manufactories for flax and shoe thread, sack and sacking manufactory, a tannery, two brick and tile works, which give employment to a great number of hands; also two quarries, yielding blue and sand stone, suitable for building purposes. Connected with Mr Oliver Magg's flax and shoe thread factory is a waterwheel about 60 feet in diameter, constructed of iron."

Sturminster Newton Mill.

COTTAGE INDUSTRIES

DORSET had many true cottage industries related to the clothing trade, but such crafts have left no field evidence. Button making (buttony) began in Shaftesbury in the 1680s and developed in the surrounding villages until Blandford became the main centre. The beautifully made buttons were much in demand by high society. Abraham Case's first buttons were 'High Tops' a disc of ram's horn with a hole in the centre and linen cone on top decorated with thread. Case and other agents had depots over much of north Dorset. The buttons were made in cottages and workhouses, and taken to the depots to be often exchanged for goods rather than money. The earlier cloth buttons were replaced by ring ones, of a special alloy made in Birmingham over which designs were threaded. In 1812, Mr Atchinson employed 1,200 women and children around Shaftesbury and the total involved is said to have been 4,000. By the 1840s the industry was in decline, and effectively killed by Ashton's button machine. Birmingham took most of the trade, causing widespread hardship which forced over 350 families to emigrate. In 1885, shirt buttons still provided employment for "a few females" at Blandford. Shaftesbury and Blandford Museums have collections of Dorset Buttons.

Wimborne and Poole were once centres of stocking making, specialising in silk and knitted woollen stockings respectively. In 1842 over 1,000 women and girls were said to be employed at Wimborne, but they could not compete with the knitting frame invented in the early nineteenth century. Stockings were made elsewhere, and according to Defoe, those at Stalbridge were the "finest, best and highest prized in the land."

Lace making was important around Blandford and Sherborne in the seventeenth century, Defoe finding bone lace from the former "as fine as any in England," while Hutchins in 1774 considered it to equal or even better that from Flanders. Lace making was introduced into Lyme Regis in the eighteenth century to allieviate hardship for women, whose skill won acclaim in a dress made for Queen Charlotte, wife of George III.

Glove making took place in Bridport in the early fifteenth century, spreading in later centuries to Beaminster, Cerne Abbas, Bere Regis, Shereborne and Blandford. Cottage outworkers finished goods for manufacturers from Somerset. Of three factories in Sherborne in 1910, the 600 employees were mainly outworkers. Today, glove making takes place in north Dorset at three factories in Gillingham and Shaftesbury which still employ outworkers.

AGRICULTURE

THIS HAS always been an important activity in such a rural county as Dorset, with arable and sheep grazing on the chalk downs, and dairying in the lusher vales and valleys. Stevenson's *General View of the Agriculture of the County* is among the more useful books giving a factual account of the agricultural scene in the early nineteenth century, while Thomas Hardy's Wessex novels paint a picture of farming at a time when mechanisation was beginning to appear on the land. In *Tess of the d'Urbervilles*, his Vales of Little Dairies and the Great Dairies, are real, in the Blackmore Vale and the Frome valley, these contrasting with the bleaker arable tracts of the chalk plateau at 'Flintcomb-Ash', believed to be the region near Piddletrenthide.

Agriculture suffered a depression in the second half of the nineteenth century, although for some farmers the railways were a godsend as they stimulated dairying in order to supply milk and dairy products to the London markets. For the industrial archaeologist, this is a good example of where two widely different industries had a common interest.

Agriculture falls uneasily within the term 'industry' in the face of more acceptable activities such as brewing or milling. With this in mind the gazetteer is concerned with agricultural monuments rather than craft tools or implements, although many of the latter are displayed at museums throughout the county. Similarly, while Dorset has many fine examples of farm buildings such as barns and dovecotes, these are arguably architectural features and so just a sample is given here. Numerous small limekilns were part of the local agricultural scene, to produce lime for spreading on the land of perhaps just one farm or estate, but these are industrial structures which deserve a separate section in the gazetteer.

Animal and water power were once prime movers on farms, and farm waterwheels are included under the agricultural heading rather than with the more usual water mills. They were used to pump water, grind animal feed, power equipment such as chaff cutters or threshing machines, and in some later cases to generate electricity. Portable horse mills, often made by local foundries, were handy as they could be moved easily about the farm for different jobs.

The later nineteenth and early twentieth centuries saw the use of the agricultural traction engine, for haulage, ploughing, threshing and sawing. Horse-drawn portable steam engines

Cider making on a Hinton St. Mary farm c. 1900.

Dorset spring wagon, Bredy Farm collection.

could also be found at work on many farms, often hired on contract. Undoubtedly the best place in the country to see many of these pre-served monsters in action is at the Dorset Steam Fair, held in the late summer every year near Blandford Forum.

Much in the way of farming tools and implements can be seen in museums. There are specialist collections, such as at Bredy Farm and Park Farm, but most museums have something on display. The rural craft collection in the Dorset County Museum (Dorchester) is a treasure trove of farming items, as varied as a wagon, smith's tools, equipment for making Dorset Blue Vinney cheese and a lever cheese press made by Pond & Son, Blandford. Cider making was once a widespread farm activity, and is commonly represented in museums. However, the best collection is in the specialist Mill House Cider Museum at Overmoigne, where the equipment can be seen in use.

Water meadows are an unusual agricultural feature, confined mostly to the chalk streams of Hampshire and Wiltshire, and here in Dorset in the Frome valley above and below Dorchester. The flooding of the water meadows in winter and early spring was controlled by a system of channels and wooden hatches. While also depositing some fertile silt, this protected the land from frost and gave an early crop of grass in the spring at a time when grazing on the downland was still poor.

Breweries, corn mills, dairies and bacon factories are among the processing industries closely associated with farming. While the first two are covered elsewhere, a good example of a bacon factory is given in the agricultural section of the gazetteer.

BREWERIES AND MALTINGS

DORSET has enjoyed a long and proud history of brewing, and its beers have been well known since the Middle Ages. In the fifteenth century, hops were imported into Poole from the Netherlands, while beer was exported to the Channel Islands. The production of malt from locally grown barley was another important activity, and this too was exported. In 1812, Stevenson recorded malt being exported to Portsmouth and London.

The prohibition of French wines during the French wars around 1700 led to the brewing of the finest malt liquors at Dorchester. The town was to maintain a reputation, for by the second half of the eighteenth century, the "best and finest beer in England" was being sent from here to London. Thomas Hardy described Dorchester's strong beer in the *Trumpet Major*, and anyone drunk and disorderly but proving to be a stranger to the town was dismissed by the magistrates "as one overtaken in a fault that no man could guard against who entered the town unawares." An especially strong Hardy's Ale is brewed at the Dorchester Brewery today. The trade with London declined, perhaps due to the cost of transport, but this was revived again when the Dorchester Brewery was built in 1880 with direct sidings from the London & South Western Railway.

Marnhull Brewery.

Before the advent of the larger breweries, many villages had their own maltings and a small brewhouse, such as at Marnhull where there were five malthouses. Cerne Abbas was noted for its malting and brewing from at least the mid-eighteenth century until the 1820s. Often, village malthouses have become houses and survive in name only (such as Malthouse Cottages at Bourton), but the Nottington malthouse is still easily recognised (site 19). The Gladwyns brewed at Litton Cheney from 1792 until about 1890. Most beer was supplied for local consumption, but some was sent to Portland, over 14 miles (22 km) away. The small brewhouse next to the brewer's cottage was still surviving in December 1988 [SY 553906]. A malthouse at nearby Barge's Farm has disappeared beneath a housing estate. It is said that the New Inn at Shipton Gorge [SY 496916] had a brewhouse in about 1830, run by the foreman of the local limekilns for his workers.

Weymouth Brewery (Devenish).

HEALTH IS EVERYTHING.

DIGESTION ASSISTED,
CHEERFULNESS PROMOTED,
ENERGY RESTORED,

BY THE USE OF

MARSH'S
Celebrated Blandford Ales,
Guaranteed Brewed only from the Finest Malt and Hops. . . . . .

See Medical Report and Analysis.

Wholesale and Retail **Wine and Spirit Merchant.**

ORDERS TO **J. L. MARSH,**
THE BREWERY, BLANDFORD.

Private houses had their own brewhouses, and there is one at Smedmore House, Kimmeridge [SY 924788]. The wall of the brewhouse at Dorchester's Colliton House has been rebuilt at the Dorset County Museum. Another museum, at Park Farm, has some items from the Milton Abbas Brewery.

For its size, Dorset has a good number of surviving breweries, and three continue in operation, at Blandford, Bridport and Dorchester. In 1889, there were thirty-two brewers in the county, but the present situation is the result of years of take-overs and amalgamations. Some long-closed town breweries have been demolished, for example Marsh's Brewery in Bryanston Street, Blandford Forum, which survived until 1986. Sherborne's brewery in Long Street was demolished and its maltings totally transformed into flats.

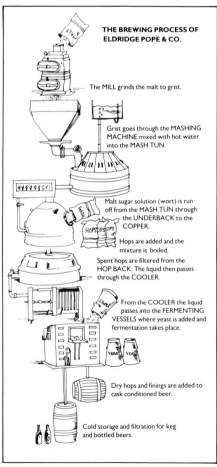

THE BREWING PROCESS OF ELDRIDGE POPE & CO.

The MILL grinds the malt to grist.

Grist goes through the MASHING MACHINE mixed with hot water into the MASH TUN.

Malt sugar solution (wort) is run off from the MASH TUN through the UNDERBACK to the COPPER.

Hops are added and the mixture is boiled.

Spent hops are filtered from the HOP BACK. The liquid then passes through the COOLER.

From the COOLER the liquid passes into the FERMENTING VESSELS where yeast is added and fermentation takes place.

Dry hops and finings are added to cask conditioned beer.

Cold storage and filtration for keg and bottled beers.

Courtesy Eldridge Pope & Co. p.l.c.

Steam Engine, Blandford Brewery.   *Hall & Woodhouse*

Ansty Brewery.   *Hall & Woodhouse*

BRICKWORKS AND POTTERIES

TODAY, there are only two brickworks in Dorset, at Godlingston near Swanage (site 29), and at Corfe Mullen, where the Beacon Hill Brick Co. makes calcium silicate (sandlime) bricks. Yet, brickmaking has taken place at about 170 sites in Dorset. Only demand and the suitability of clays determined the size of operations, and products included bricks, tiles and agricultural drainpipes. Clays of several different geological periods produced distinctly coloured bricks. Over a hundred brickworks were concentrated in south-east Dorset, around Poole and Bournemouth, where sanitary wares were also produced. Some became large mechanised works after the mid-nineteenth century when the railways could bring in coals. There was an ambitious scheme on Brownsea Island in the 1850s, making bricks, sewage pipes and terra cotta. The 1960s and 70s saw many closures, due to competition from modern plants and the revolution caused by plastic pipes. The clay pits became restricted by encroaching urban development, beneath which many of the sites have now disappeared. One of the last was the Sandford works, which was a familiar landmark beside the A351 one mile (1.6 km) north of Wareham, but all trace has gone beneath a housing estate.

There was a group of brickworks around Weymouth, where the growth of the resort was a ready market. Brickmaking took place at Broadmayne village until the Second World War, producing the familiar speckled bricks seen in Dorchester. Bridport in the west had brickworks, while there were scattered works throughout north Dorset. Some large country estates had their own brickyards, such as at Charborough Park where there is a remarkable

Chickerell Brickworks.

2 mile (3.2 km) brick wall beside the A31. It was built in about 1840 at the same time as the turnpike road.

Physical evidence may be difficult to find, and to use rural north Dorset as an example, the only evidence may be a place name, such as Brickyard Cottages near Stourton Caundle. Brickyard Lane at Bourton is another clue. Here, a shallow clay pit is now overgrown, while one of the larger pits at Gillingham is now a fishing pond. The Gillingham works were demolished to make way for an industrial estate, but towards Shaftesbury a long drying shed at the Hawker's Hill (Motcombe) brickworks has been incorporated in a farm.

Bricks are always interesting when they have a name or initials stamped on them as this often gives their origin. For example, 'R.English, King Stagg' conveniently gives the brickmaker's name too. Being on the Westminster estate, bricks from Motcombe were stamped 'W'. The letter 'G' is also found in the district, perhaps representing Grosvenor, the family name of the Westminsters. John Hussey's bricks at Marnhull were stamped 'H' from the 1850s until 1901.

Despite the working and export of clays at nearby Purbeck and Wareham, there was no large scale pottery production in the Poole district until the second half of the nineteenth century. The Patent Architectural Pottery Co was established at Hamworthy in 1854, making coloured and glazed bricks, mouldings and wall tiles. Cornish china clay was added to the local raw material. The Kinson Pottery was begun at a similar time, and made drain pipes and terra cotta goods.

As with brickmaking in the area, the potteries closed, but the well known Poole Pottery has survived (site 26) as a highly modern operation. This East Quay Works was begun in about 1860 by James Walker who made floor tiles. It was bought out by Jesse Carter in 1873. The Carters took over the Architectural Pottery at Hamworthy in 1895 and the two factories specialised in floor and wall tiles and decorative pottery. Examples of painted wares from early this century can be seen in the museum of the Poole Pottery. Just along the Quay, the front of the Poole Arms is a fine example of green glazed wall tiles.

Two potteries making coarseware were recorded at Beaminster in 1812, but Dorset's most remarkable potteries were the small rural ones collectively known as the Verwood potteries. Potting began at Alderholt in the early fourteenth century. It was well established by the seventeenth and eighteenth centuries, when small groups were exploiting the clay deposits from Alderholt south-west to Horton, with Verwood at the centre. All types of practical earthenware were made, mostly sold by hawkers who ranged up to 40 miles (64 km) from the kilns. The industry declined in the nineteenth century through competition from mass produced wares. The Cross Roads kiln at Verwood was the last to close, in 1952. The brick-lined kilns were about 10 feet (3 m) high, surrounded by a mound of earth, clay and broken pots. The Verwood & District Potteries Trust was formed in 1985 to record and preserve the remaining evidence of the potteries. There are good collections of Verwood pottery in the museums at Christchurch, Dorchester and Poole.

CLAY

THERE IS evidence of ball clay working – past and present – to the south of Wareham, but particularly along the foot of the Purbeck Hills ridge. Back in 1650 there was a demand for clay for tobacco pipes and in the eighteenth and nineteenth centuries clay was exported to the Minton and Wedgwood potteries. Doulton & Co. had clay pits, but the main development was by Benjamin Fayle and Pike Brothers. Both built their own tramways to Middlebere, Goathorn and Ridge quays on Poole Harbour, and these are now part of the archaeology of this industry (sites 107 and 108). In 1812, up to 20,000 tons of clay was being shipped to Liverpool for the Staffordshire potteries. Export rose to 69,286 tons in 1851. An increasing proportion was used in the pottery and tile works established around Poole in the second half of the century. The two main clay firms merged in 1948 to become Pike Brothers, Fayle & Co. Ltd.

Purbeck clay mine

Output today is about 200,000 tons, from pits and mines managed by ECC Ball Clays. It must be Dorset's least seen extractive industry, for the sites are well screened by trees. One example is Squirrel Cottage Pit, worked since about 1979. The overburden of sands must be removed to gain the seam of clay which is dug by an excavator to a depth of 15 feet (4.6 m). Lorries take the two types of clay to the Furzebrook depot. The clay is also worked in drift mines, on a small scale and well concealed at the surface. Probably the most visible is at Norden near Corfe Castle. The Greenspecks Mine is different. From the raised shed at the surface

Clay pit at Corfe.

which houses storage bins and a powerful winch, a 22 inch gauge tramway descends a 1 in 6 incline into the mouth of the mine, surrounded by a dense tree cover – an almost fairy tale mine. The foot of the incline is 120 feet (36 m) below surface, and three teams of two men work the seam of 'Prima' or 'No.1' clay. They use pneumatic tools with spade-like bits to extract the clay and leave a thick layer to form a watertight roof. When ready, trains of loaded clay waggons are winched out of the mine to the surface.

Furzebrook, the former headquarters of Pike Brothers, is the main processing depot where clay is brought for storage and processing from the half dozen or so mines and pits. The clay is shredded and blended into about twenty-five grades, and bagged at the modern plant. The main use for Purbeck's clay is for the pottery industry, but other grades are used as fillers in synthetic rubber, fertilizers and animal feeds.

STONE QUARRYING

WHEREVER THERE is stone there are old quarries, for quarrying for building stone was a major industry in Dorset. They are mostly in the Jurassic limestones of Dorset's varied geology, on Portland and Purbeck, but also around Bridport (Bothenhampton) and Sherborne. An oolitic freestone was quarried around Marnhull, similar to Bath stone. As with the limestones, chalk was often quarried for limeburning. Over-

grown workings extend along the escarpments around Shaftesbury, where the Upper Greensand was quarried for centuries for local building stone. A harder greensand known as rag was quarried for cobbles and roadstone as well as building. There are sand and gravel pits in south-east Dorset.

The famous Portland quarries furnished stone for Wren's St Paul's Cathedral, and centuries of quarrying have left their mark on the island, which has a unique landscape scarred with old workings. Small shipping points along the east coast and the Merchants Railway (site 109) are part of the industrial archaeology here. The latter was built in 1826 to ease transport when 25,000 tons of stone were being shipped every year. In 1839, there were fifty-six quarries employing 240 men. 1899 was a peak year with 1,441 quarrymen and masons, although 820 of these were employed on the Breakwater extension scheme. Today, about a hundred are employed in the industry.

The Isle of Purbeck was famed for the quarrying and fashioning of Purbeck marble in the Middle Ages. Corfe Castle became the centre for manufacturing cathedral and church fittings, such as pillars, tomb slabs and fonts, until the stone fell out of fashion with the introduction of alabaster for carving effigies. But in the nineteenth and early twentieth centuries, much of Purbeck's stone was worked underground. A Portland type of stone was worked in galleries along the cliffs from Tilly Whim to Winspit, while on the high ground between Swanage and Worth Matravers, through Langton Matravers

St. Aldhelm's Quarry.

Horse whim in a Purbeck stone quarry.

and Acton, there were seams of hard stone worked from inclined shafts. These had a horse worked capstan at the top to haul up the stone trucks. A few sites can be seen today, such as the wild area above Swanage known as the Townsend Nature Reserve which is pitted with old workings and shafts [SZ 024783]. The two 'crab stones' which held the capstan may now be the only clue, standing beside a shallow depression as at SZ 018781. In 1907, there were 197 men working in fifty-eight stone mines. Swanage developed as a place of export before it became better known as a tourist resort. Stone kerbs and setts were stacked along the shoreline awaiting shipment to London until the 1880s.

With two exceptions, the gazetteer concentrates on the quarries of Portland and Purbeck. Both districts have museums with exhibits on the stone industry: the Portland Museum at Wakeham, and the Tithe Barn Museum at Swanage. The stone museum at Langton Matravers merits its own description.

OTHER MINERAL WORKINGS

APART FROM water power, the growth of Dorset's industries was always inhibited by the lack of fuel, especially once steam power was introduced. There were attempts to find coal in

the eighteenth century around Sherborne and Shaftesbury, and a borehole of 1,300 feet (396 m) was sunk at Lyme Regis in 1901. All failed, but the so-called Kimmeridge Coal was the most promising. This bituminous shale was used by cottagers for fuel and was exploited commercially on several occasions. Of all industrial sites, Kimmeridge is the one of the most fascinating, especially the evidence of oil shale extraction in the nineteenth century (sites 44 and 126). At the turn of the century, the Kimmeridge Oil & Carbon Co claimed the Blackstone Seam yielded 120 gallons of paraffin per ton. The remaining coke and carbon was used as a disinfectant and fertiliser. There is a modern industry here too, for on the other side of the bay stands the 'nodding donkey' pump and well head of the 1959 oil find. Oil shale was also worked at Portesham and Corton. The Portesham quarries (site 35) overlook the overgrown remains of the Manfield Shale Pit, which had a small engine house in 1901 [SY 609856]. Shale oil at Westham, Weymouth, proved uneconomical.

Other minerals had all the potential of a chemical industry for Dorset, but no attempt was very successful.

Alum was extracted from alum stone or bituminous shale by boiling. It was used in preparing mordants in dyeing and calico-printing, preserving skins, candle making, and pharmacy. In the early seventeenth century Sir William Clavell spent £4000 on an alum works and a pier at Kimmeridge, but this soon closed when others

Kimmeridge shale quarry.

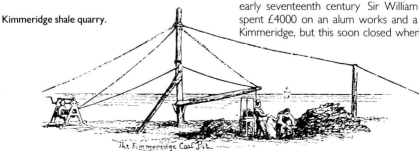

The Kimmeridge Coal Pit

were granted the king's patent to manufacture alum. Clavell then had little luck in setting up salt works, and a glasshouse which worked in 1617-23 using Kimmeridge coal as a fuel. The furnace was destroyed after an attempt to break the monopoly which prevented sales beyond the local area.

Copperas, or green vitriol, was prepared by dissolving decomposing iron pyrites in rain water or dilute sulphuric acid. This important salt was used by tanners while dyers used it to make Prussian blue. In the late seventeenth century, stones were collected from the beach of Brownsea Island, dissolved and boiled in vats. At a similar time, Sir Richard Clayton's works at Studland used stones from the Isle of Wight.

Gypsum has been worked on a small scale at Durlston Bay, Purbeck. In the nineteenth century, ironstone was worked commercially at Hengistbury Head (site 43), then in Hampshire, but a vein at Abbotsbury proved to contain too much silica to be economic.

LIMEKILNS

LIMEBURNING in kilns was common in most limestone and chalk districts, producing lime for building mortars but mostly for spreading on farmland. Broken stone and fuel were loaded in the top of the kiln in alternate layers, being replenished to allow continuous burning, and the burnt lime extracted from the drawhole at the bottom. A country kiln such as at Church Knowle (site 46) had a capacity for 5½ tons of chalk and 2 tons of coal, yielding 4 tons of quicklime. In 1812, coal and culm for burning

limestone were imported "to a considerable extent", so examples on the shore at Lulworth Cove and Charmouth were conveniently placed for importing fuel.

Shillingstone chalk pit

Many limekilns were small agricultural ones alongside a small quarry, frequently at lonely sites. Among the exceptions is a small kiln actually among the buildings at Grigg Farm [SY 504928] which can be seen from the A35 about 3 miles (4.8 km) east of Bridport. Of a more modern age, the disused chalk quarry at Whitesheet Hill, near Maiden Newton, has two limekilns built of concrete blocks [SY 586980]. Now overgrown, these were last worked by Soil Fertility Ltd. The last limekilns still at work in the county are at Shillingstone, another chalk quarry (site 50).

Ordnance Survey 25 inch maps of the turn of the century show great concentrations of kilns in some areas, but not all have survived the intervening years. Those that remain are too numerous to list individually, so a small selection is given in the gazetteer.

Church Knowle limekiln.

Langton Herring limekiln.

FOUNDRIES AND ENGINEERING WORKS

GOOD EVIDENCE for the existence of foundries in many small towns in Dorset comes from their cast ironwork. The maker's name (and sometimes the date) may be cast upon such varied products as agricultural implements, drain gratings, roadsigns, sluices or waterwheels, all of which can be found throughout the county.

Poole Foundry, which backed onto Poole Quay, was the last of the jobbing foundries in the town and closed in 1985. The site was cleared for residential development, a fate met by other Poole foundries including Stephen Lewin's earlier Poole Foundry (1841-84) which is now South Road School. Among the products of his foundry, Lewin made steam launches and railway locomotives. Customers for the latter included the Guinness Brewery in Dublin. An early locomotive was in use at Seaham harbour, Durham, until 1969 and has been preserved. More locally, the foundry made the locomotive *Tiny* for Fayle's Goathorn clay railway in 1868. It was scrapped in 1948.

There were small town foundries and agricultural engineers, such as Farris of Shaftesbury, or Pond of Blandford. Dorchester had important foundries, of which Lott & Walne was the last to close. This firm made agricultural equipment and street furniture, but specialised in water carts which were often sold outside the county. Within Dorset, their drain gratings went as far north as Shaftesbury, where the local foundry of John Farris also made them. The Grove Iron Works remains a working foundry just outside Bridport. The works buildings are alongside a stone house close to the main road at West Allington.

Outsiders found their way into Dorset too, such as E. Cockey & Sons of Frome, who supplied the cast iron pillars for the main gallery at the Dorset County Museum in 1883. Their name also appears on the cast iron mileposts along the A30 around Shaftesbury. Another Somerset foundry, Dening & Co. of Chard, supplied agricultural machinery and cast iron tombstones. Joseph Armfield of Ringwood, Hampshire, was a supplier of milling equipment such as turbines and sluices.

Another side of engineering was the blacksmith's and wheelwright's shop, found in many small communities when horse-drawn wagons were the main method of rural transport. One such shop fortunately survives at South Perrott.

Lott & Walne Foundry.

West Mill, Bridport.

MILLS

SPACE PERMITS just a sample from Dorset's rich heritage of watermills, for there are several hundred mills or sites recorded in the county. Many mills are on ancient sites mentioned in the Domesday Book; after successive rebuildings, milling is still taking place at a few. These are corn or grist mills, as farm and industrial mills are described elsewhere. Every river was harnessed, and an interesting way to study Dorset's mills is to follow just one river from source to sea. The Stour is a particularly rewarding example. Restoration has taken place at several mills in recent years and there is an increasing number open to the public.

According to the nature of the stream, there are all types of waterwheel from undershot to overshot, of particular interest when the maker's name and date may be cast. A small waterwheel might drive two pairs of stones and other machinery. This includes a sack hoist to take corn to bins in the top of the building from where it feeds by gravity to the stones on the milling floor. The bagging of flour takes place on the ground floor. Around the turn of the cen-

tury, several mills were converted to more efficient turbine power, usually supplied by Joseph Armfield of Ringwood. Such an example is Sturminster Newton Mill (site 64) where the turbine has been working since 1904.

The first reference to a windmill in Dorset was in 1267, at Buckhorn Weston. This was probably of the post mill type. Only two windmills survive in Dorset, from perhaps thirty sites. These are tower mills, both on Portland and in good condition (site 63). Place names are a clue to the former existence of others, such as Windmill Hill, at Packers Hill near Kingstag [**ST 717106**] and Windmill Barrow, south-west of Sturminster Marshall [**SY 937977**]. There was at least one at Poole, permitted by an Act of 1543.

Melbury Abbas Mill.

TEXTILES

ALTHOUGH the sheep of the Dorset downs had always supplied fleece, the westcountry woollen textile industry only just reached down into the county. Locally grown flax was important for linen in some parts. In the early seventeenth century, broadcloth from Dorchester was exported to France, but it was mostly produced for local use. In the eighteenth century, swanskin was made in the district around Shaftesbury and Sturminster Newton, the latter employing over 1,200 people in 1812. Swanskin was a coarse white flannel used for soldiers' clothing and Newfoundland fishermen. Dowlas (a coarse linen) and bed ticking were made at Gillingham and Silton, while some dowlas was also made at Cerne Abbas. Linen cloth was made at Bourton, where three quarters of the population were in the weaving industry in the early nineteenth century. Locally grown flax was supplemented by yarn imported from Holland. Sailcloth and sacking were produced in Beaminster, where the church has a carving of a wool merchant's sign.

Flax and hemp were grown between the coast at Bridport and Beaminster since at least Saxon times. After harvesting, bundles of flax were placed in water for about a fortnight to separate the fibres from the rest. Once dried, a later process was called swingling and involved removing broken straw. The flax was next separated into parallel fibres by heckling. Richard Roberts erected an early flax swingling mill at Burton Bradstock in 1803, while spinning took place downstream at his Grove Mill.

Bridport was the main centre for rope and net making in Dorset. In 1211, a thousand yards of sail cloth and hempen ships' cables were ordered, and two years later King John ordered as many ropes as possible. This was the beginning of a long connection with the navy, which only diminished when ropewalks were set up at the royal dockyards. In 1793, it was estimated that 1,800 in Bridport and over 7,000 in the neighbourhood were making everything from small ropes to ships' cables. By 1812, the district was producing all sorts of twine, string, packthread, netting, cordage and ropes. This included the finest thread used by saddlers, huge cables for warships, and nets for the New-

Braiding nets at Eype near Bridport in 1913.

A jumper loom dating from 1860. *Bridport Museum.*

foundland fishery. The Hounsell and Gundry families were prominent in the industry since the early seventeenth century, the latter at Court, Grove and Pymore. By then two-thirds of the flax and hemp was being imported from places such as Riga on the Baltic. It was cleaned by combers, spun into twine on wheels turned by children, and twisted on broad rope walks, where the machines were turned by boys while the men walked back to draw out the twisting threads. Much of the net making was done by outworkers, the twine being taken to women cottagers who braided the nets. Carpet thread was sent to Kidderminster.

After amalgamations, the Hounsells became Bridport Industries Ltd, which combined with Joseph Gundry & Co in 1963 to form Bridport Gundry Ltd, still the major employer. Modern technology and artificial fibres are now used.

Bridport's distinctive industry of rope and net making has left a number of industrial buildings, many of which are no longer used in the trade. Most survivals are of the late nineteenth and early twentieth centuries and include spinning mills, covered walks for rope and twine spinning, weaving or net-making sheds, warehouses and office blocks. Nearby Pymore is a notable village and factory site.

There were silk mills in north Dorset, at Sherborne and Gillingham, and 400 were said to be employed in the industry in 1765. Westbury Mill at Sherborne was a grist mill converted to silk throwing by John Sharrer of Whitechapel. His nephew, William Willmott became manager in 1769, when Italian and Spanish silk winding machines were used. The business later changed to weaving and continued until the 1950s. The Gillingham Silk Co. was established in about 1769 next to the Town Mill. The workforce of 150 included girl apprentices from London workhouses, who slept in a dormitory in a nearby building. The business closed in 1895 and all trace has gone. Part was incorporated in the Town Mill, but this had a fire and after a long period of uncertainty, it was demolished in 1988 to build houses. There were smaller silk mills at Cerne Abbas, Stalbridge and Marnhull.

ROADS

AS WITH most counties, roads were in a poor state until the turnpike trusts of the second half of the eighteenth century. Even so, in 1812 Stevenson described some lesser roads in the Blackmore Vale and west Dorset as "miry, and scarcely passable in winter, and the large rough loose stones with which they abound render them very unpleasant in summer." The turnpike trusts were set up by Acts to collect tolls to improve and maintain Dorset's main roads. Their effect was to fix the road pattern for the future. The first was the Shaftesbury & Sherborne Trust (1753-4), along the present A30, followed immediately by the Harnham, Blandford & Dorchester Trust, now the A354. The Maiden Newton Trust (1777-8) was one of the most important in central Dorset. The Vale of Blackmoor Trust gained its name in 1824-5, although it had been established sixty years earlier. This and most others had branch roads, some crossing into other counties. The Puddletown & Wimborne Trust came late, in 1840, and was followed by the last trust consisting of a bridge and short road at Weymouth in 1857. In all, there were twenty trusts. Some had been abandoned by 1888 when the new county council became responsible for the main roads. Dorset's roads offer much of interest to the traveller with a keen eye. Examples of bridges ranging in date from the Middle Ages to the twentieth century are included here. Some Dorset bridges have cast iron notices, reading:

DORSET
ANY PERSON WILFULLY INJURING
ANY PART OF THIS COUNTY BRIDGE
WILL BE GUILTY OF FELONY AND
UPON CONVICTION LIABLE TO BE
TRANSPORTED FOR LIFE
BY THE COURT
7 & 8 GEO 4 C30 S13   T.FOOKS

Fooks was Clerk of the Peace, and the details of this Act of 1828 state that anyone convicted could be "transported beyond the Seas for Life, or for any Term not exceeding Four Years; and, if a Male, to be once, twice, or thrice publicly or privately whipped (if the Court shall so think fit), in addition to such Imprisonment." These were hard times and just six years before the famous Tolpuddle Martyrs were transported for form-

Charminster tollhouse.

Milepost, Charminster.

Museum, while there is a fourth in Salisbury Museum. Milestones can be seen along the main highways, although the sequence may be incomplete. They may be stones with carved letters and numbers, stones with cast iron plates, or cast iron mileposts, all in varying styles according to the turnpike trust. A small selection only is given here. The characteristic Dorset guideposts with circular finials, giving a place name and grid reference, are widespread. They only date from about 1948-64, and were made of cast aluminium by the Royal Label Factory at Stratford-upon-Avon. The first to be erected was at Hell Corner, near Yetminster.

Miscellaneous street furniture includes post-boxes, lamp posts, fountains, and water troughs. Dorset can claim the earliest letter box still in use in England, at Barnes Cross. One in Dorchester's South Walks is also early, but there are numerous other Victorian examples. An early 'K 1' telephone kiosk is also included in the gazetteer because of its rarity.

Twentieth century public transport vehicles, in the form of buses, trams and trolley buses are well represented at the Bournemouth Transport Museum (site 85). Of related interest, an iron turning plate in the old trolley bus terminus can be seen in a redeveloped courtyard off Church Lane in Christchurch.

ing a secret farm workers' union. The transportation notice removed from Wareham's old Frome bridge in 1927 is in the Dorset County Museum, but others can be seen in place on several bridges. There are other cast iron notices, some which warn traction engine drivers of bridges which are "insufficient to carry weights beyond the ordinary traffic of the district." As well as bridges, there are two notable tunnels in the west of the county.

Dorset finial signpost. *J. Johns*

Single or two storey tollhouses can be seen along former turnpike roads, although many have been demolished or so altered to be difficult to recognise. The one at Charminster (site 88) is particularly fine. A tollboard of the Vale of Blackmoor Trust can be seen on a tollhouse beside the A357 at South Cheriton [ST 693248], just outside the county in Somerset. Boards from the Madjeston and Perns Mill gates of the same trust can be seen in Gillingham

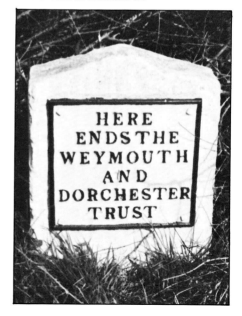

RAILWAYS FOR INDUSTRY

Narrow gauge railway at Norden clay mine, 1968

THE FIRST railways or tramways in Dorset served the clay and stone industries of Purbeck and Portland. These were self-contained systems, of sufficient interest to be distinguished from the main line networks. Most were horse-worked, although steam locomotives were later introduced in Purbeck on the Goathorn Tramway and the Pike Tramway to Ridge Quay, both for carrying clay. The Fayle Tramway from Norden to Middlebere Quay was completed in 1806, and was thus one of the earliest in southern England. Purbeck also had tramways at Kimmeridge, Swanage Pier, and Cocknowle where an incline served chalk and marl pits. The Merchants' Railway of 1826 had an impressive incline down to Castleton from the top of Portland.

There were other industrial tramways in Dorset, not included in the gazetteer, such as one of about a mile (1.6 km) connecting the pier and clay pits with the brick, pipe and terra cotta works on Brownsea Island in the 1850s. Other brickyards had internal tramways, where the clay pits were some distance away. For example, the Gillingham brick and tile works had a diesel hauled narrow gauge tramway in the later years until closure in 1968.

RAILWAYS

THE PRINCIPAL railway monuments in Dorset include stations, bridges, viaducts and tunnels, while cuttings and embankments should not be forgotten along some stretches of track. The effect of the railways was to bring increased traffic and prosperity to those towns which lay on their routes. Two formerly important towns, Cerne Abbas and Beaminster, were missed by the railways, and both declined in population thereafter.

Still in use are the two east-west London & South Western Railway (LSWR) lines through north and south Dorset, the latter from Bournemouth to Dorchester, and the north-south Great Western Railway (GWR) line from Yeovil to Weymouth. The other north-south route, the Somerset & Dorset Joint Railway, is closed but much of its course can be traced. This is also true of the branches to Lyme Regis (mostly in Devon!), Bridport, Abbotsbury and Portland. However, parts of the Swanage line are open, including the restored Swanage Railway.

The first main line in Dorset was the Southampton & Dorchester Railway, opened in 1847 and taken over by the LSWR in the following year. It entered the county via Ringwood, Wimborne and Wareham, a circuitous route which gained it the name "Castleman's Corkscrew" after the Wimborne solicitor who was the chief promoter. Dorchester South Station pointed west as there were plans to extend the line to Fal-

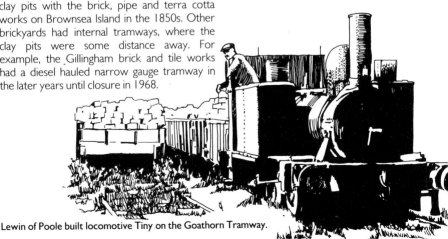

Lewin of Poole built locomotive Tiny on the Goathorn Tramway.

Maiden Newton Station in 1964.

mouth, but the main line curved south to share the Great Western line to Weymouth. For many years up trains had to reverse into the station, the remains of which is now within the Dorchester brewery site. Poole was served by a branch to Hamworthy, until there was a direct line from Broadstone in 1872. The Salisbury & Dorset Junction Railway came to West Moors from Fordingbridge via Alderholt and Verwood in 1861. Bournemouth resisted the railways for a long part of its development, and was approached by lines from Poole (west) and Christchurch (east). Only in 1888 were the two lines connected to form the present through route from Waterloo to Weymouth.

The LSWR had a second line, the Salisbury & Yeovil Railway (1859-6), which passes in and out of north Dorset. This is still the main line from Waterloo to Exeter, with stations at Gillingham and Sherborne.

The Wiltshire, Somerset & Weymouth Railway (later, GWR) reached Weymouth via Yeovil and Dorchester in 1857. I.K. Brunel was the engineer of this broad gauge line. The whole of the Frome valley section has numerous bridges and tunnels of interest. Until 1874, the track from Dorchester to Weymouth was mixed gauge as there was a junction with the LSWR. The planned railway routes at Dorchester would have destroyed Maumbury Rings and Poundbury hillfort, but when faced by protest, it was agreed to avoid the former, and to tunnel at greater cost beneath the latter. The cut-and-cover tunnel at Frampton was not so much to

preserve the landscape, but to maintain hunting rights across the route.

The much loved Somerset & Dorset Joint Railway, which brought thousands of holiday makers to Poole and Bournemouth from the Midlands via Bath, was an amalgamation of the Dorset Central and Somerset Central Railways in 1875. The former was built from Wimborne to Blandford in 1860, and extended to Bruton in Somerset two years later. The line was closed in 1966 (although a short length to Blandford remained for freight until 1969), but its course can be traced over the Blackmore Vale and through the Stour valley. On the site of Blandford Forum station (now flats) a buffer-stop is preserved beneath the original footbridge.

Dorset's five main branch lines were all to the coast. The Bridport branch (1857–1975) was built as a broad gauge line from the GWR at Maiden Newton. An extension was made to the harbour and potential resort of West Bay in 1884 by which time the line was standard gauge. This closed in 1930. There are some remains through the hills around Toller Porcorum and Powerstock. Level crossing gates and rails across a road are preserved at Bradpole The Swanage branch was opened in May 1885 from the LSWR at Wareham to Swanage, and saw much summer holiday traffic to the resort, as well as local passengers and the export of clay. When it closed in 1972 the track was only retained to Furzebrook where clay and oil traffic continued. The Swanage Railway (site 121) is now being relaid, to restore a passenger service and relieve congestion on Purbeck's roads.

The Weymouth & Portland Railway (1865–1965) was run by the GWR and LSWR. Works involved cuttings and embankments, and viaducts across the Backwater and Fleet. The line served the island and the naval base. An extension, the Easton & Church Hope Railway, was authorised in 1867 but not opened until 1900. It climbed to the top of the island around the east side where there was a long cutting. Much stone traffic came from Easton, but landslips closed the line on at least two occasions.

The Abbotsbury branch (1885–1952) from the GWR at Broadwey near Weymouth was no match for road transport. Mineral traffic was never great, although an incline was laid to the Portesham quarries (site 35).

The Lyme Regis Railway (1903–1965) was a branch from the LSWR at Axminster in Devon. Only the last few yards were in Dorset, arriving at Lyme Regis station at 250 feet (76m) above sea level. The wooden station building now serves as a shop at Alresford Station of the Mid-Hants Railway. The spectacular concrete Cannington viaduct is in Devon, but worth a visit.

There were two short military branches, both about 2 miles (3.6 km) long and in use for a few years after the Great War: from Blandford to Blandford Camp and from Wool to Bovington Camp.

The S.S. Nerma discharging hemp from the Baltic at Bridport c.1900.   *Bridport Museum*

PORTS AND SHIPPING

DORSET has a long maritime tradition, with activity at ports from Lyme Regis in the west to Poole Harbour in the east. Christchurch Harbour, formerly in Hampshire, is now included too. Warehouses are part of the quayside scene at Weymouth and Poole. In addition to a mixed trade, the former developed as a ferry port to France and the Channel Islands. Since the seventeenth century, Poole was associated with the Newfoundland fisheries trade for about 150 years. Bridport completed the Dorset connection with Newfoundland, finding a good market for its nets here. Wooden shipbuilding for local owners took place at Dorset ports, notably at Bridport and Hamworthy (Poole).

Shipping was not just concerned with the ports, for the stone quarrying industry had exposed loading places with cliffside cranes on the east side of Portland and along the Purbeck coast. Short-lived piers were built as a result of industrial activities on the open coast at Kimmeridge. Small piers on the south side of Poole Harbour, at Ridge, Middlebere and Goathorn, were used for loading Purbeck ball clay into barges which carried it to larger ships at Poole.

There is another side to shipping too. By their purpose, lighthouses are conspicuous and impressive monuments – especially the one at Portland Bill – and are thus included in the gazetteer. There are other miscellaneous sites of related maritime interest, such as coastguard houses and lookouts. St Aldhelm's Head is a notable example.

UTILITIES

THE WATER, gas and electricity supply industries all became increasingly important as urban development progressed throughout the country in the nineteenth and twentieth centuries.

Wimborne Waterworks pumping station.

Of the first, the works in Dorset are mostly pumping stations for extracting water from rivers, springs or deep boreholes within the porous chalk. The Sutton Poyntz site of the Weymouth Waterworks Co. was authorised by an Act of 1855, and is described in the gazetteer. Elsewhere in the district is the more recent Friar Wadden Pumping Station, a bright red brick building in a valley near Upwey. In Purbeck, the Corfe Castle pumping station of 1921 is in Purbeck stone, and stands beside the Studland road near the railway viaduct. At Ulwell near Swanage, a conspicuous granite obelisk on Ballard Down was erected in 1892 by George Burt to commemorate the success of the waterworks below. It once stood supporting a gas lamp in London, but was brought to Swanage in a returning stone boat as were so many other redundant items. The archaeology of water supply includes the many spouts, taps and pumps which can be seen in Dorset towns and villages, although these can be classed as street furniture.

The Bournemouth & District Water Co. was founded in 1862 as the Bournemouth Gas & Water Co. and continued to supply both commodities until 1949 when the gas was nationalised. The earlier water extraction sites included Walford and Longham, with a water treatment plant and reservoir at Alderney. After producing gas at Bourne Valley, oper-

ations were transferred to the Poole gas works on Poole Quay at the turn of the century.

The first gas works in Dorset was at Bridport (site 138), which began producing town gas from coal in 1832. The cast iron horizontal retorts were supplied by the Neath Abbey Iron Co. Gas was first used for street lighting, but domestic lights, cookers and heaters became more common in the 1850s. There were other gas works at Beaminster, Gillingham, Lyme Regis, Shaftesbury, Sherborne, Stalbridge and Sturminster Newton. Unusually, the Weymouth gas works was built and run by W.W.Burdon in 1836–67, before being taken over by the Weymouth Gas Consumers Co. Ltd. The site was enlarged in 1933 on reclaimed land. The gas works in the small towns were closed when connected to the grid main from Poole, but even that large works succumbed when natural gas was introduced. Like the others which served their communities so well, it has been demolished. Sherborne Museum contains a small No.5 Alcazer steam engine (E.S.Hindley & Son of Bourton, 1925) which drove tar and liquid pumps at the works of the Sherborne Gas & Coke Co. Coal gas was not alone in Dorset, for there was a plant in Wareham using Kimmeridge shale to produce gas for street lights in the 1840s and 50s.

Poole can claim Dorset's most conspicuous industrial monument in its power station, at present redundant but not yet part of industrial archaeology. It was commissioned in 1951 as a coal-fired station, but was converted to oil in the 1970s. Nearby Christchurch has the comprehensive Wedgwood Electrical Collection (site 145). On a smaller scale, an interesting item in the museum at Blandford Forum is a fully restored dynamo which supplied the first domestic electricity in the town.

Bridport Power Station.

LOCATION OF SITES IN GAZETTEER

------- COUNTY BOUNDARY
++++++++++ RAILWAYS
~~~~ RIVERS
───── MAIN ROADS

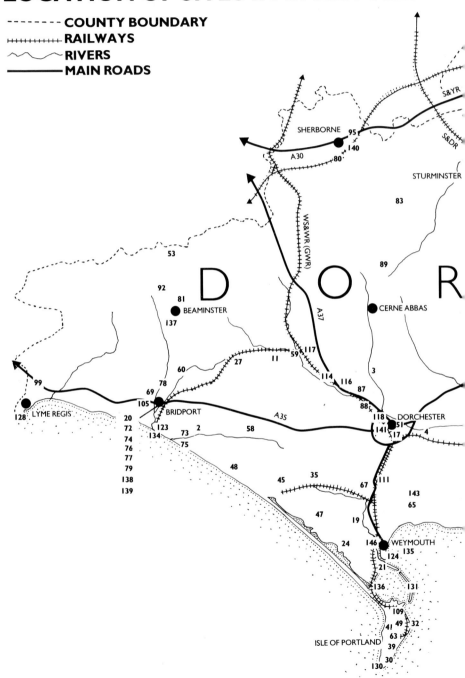

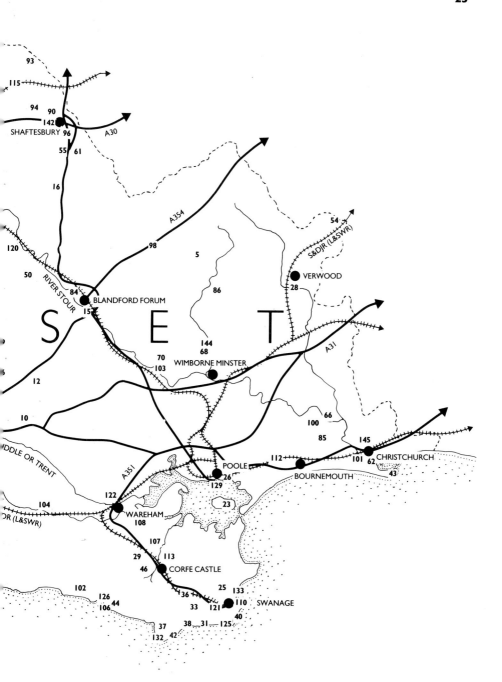

93
115
94
90
142
SHAFTESBURY 96
55 61
A30
16
A354
98
54
S&DJR (L&SWR)
120
5
50
RIVER STOUR
VERWOOD
86
28
84
15
BLANDFORD FORUM
S   E   T
144
68
70
103
WIMBORNE MINSTER
A31
12
66
10
100
85
145
112
101 62
CHRISTCHURCH
IDDLE OR TRENT
POOLE
26
129
BOURNEMOUTH
43
A351
23
122
104
WAREHAM
DR (L&SWR)
108
107
29 113
46
CORFE CASTLE
102
25 133
126
136
110 SWANAGE
106 44
33 121
40
38 31 125
37
132 42

GAZETTEER

This gazetteer describes a personal choice of the more visible sites throughout Dorset. Many can be visited, either as a public attraction or by courtesy of the owner; at the very least they can be seen from a road, footpath, railway, or even the sea as in the case of the cliffside quarries in Purbeck. They can be found by using the numbered location map and the Ordnance Survey 1:50,000 map, although the enthusiast will find the larger scale 1:25,000 map gives much greater detail. Access is seldom denied, so always ask permission to enter property whenever in doubt. It is worth remembering that many places which open to the public may only do so during the summer months. Most local museums have something of industrial interest relating to their district, and reference to some is given in the gazetteer.

AGRICULTURE

ATHELHAMPTON DOVECOTE
[SY 770942]   **I**

Dating from the early fifteenth century, this circular dovecote is believed to be the oldest of several examples in Dorset. It is of stone, beneath a conical tile and stone-slate roof, and contains some 600 pigeon holes. It is just north-west of Athelhampton Hall near Puddletown, and is open to the public. ☎ 030 584 363.

BREDY FARM COLLECTION
[SY 507899]   **2**

This is a working farm in the attractive Bride valley to the east of Burton Bradstock, and the collection includes old farming tools and other equipment. Traditional Dorset wagons are among the horse-drawn items. Cider making takes place here and there is a working sawmill, using a horizontal reciprocating saw formerly at Mangerton Mill. An iron waterwheel, by Winter & Hossey of Dorchester, is awaiting restoration.

FORSTON FARM WHEEL
[SY 666955]   **3**

A low breast shot wheel, 16' × 5' 6" (4·8m × 1·7m), which once drove via a long shaft a pump, saw, millstones, and a milking machine. It is in the open, and can be seen across the Cerne river from the A352, one mile (1·6km) south of Godmanstone.

FROME VALLEY WATER MEADOWS
[SY 717907]   **4**

The Frome valley above and below Dorchester has many traces of abandoned ditches, sluices and low arched bridges. They can be seen from most roads which cross the valley. A system is being restored by the Dorset Agricultural College at Kingston Maurward, and can be seen from the pretty streamside footpath to Dorchester, two fields west of the bridge at Lower Bockhampton.

GUSSAGE SHEEP DIP
[ST 994110]   **5**

A well preserved sheep dip, brick lined and oval shaped with iron grooves for the hatch boards. It makes use of the stream immediately behind the Bournemouth & District Water Co.'s borehole site where the Ackling Dyke (Roman road) bridleway meets the valley road near Gussage All Saints.

Gussage sheep dip.

HEWISH FARM WHEEL, MILTON ABBAS
[ST 806001]   **6**

An iron wheel, 21' × 4' 2" (6·4m × 1·27m), made by Hossey of Dorchester, with a ring gear drive by Lott & Walne. It once drove farm machinery in a barn via a long shaft, and a generator until the 1960s. Now under restoration, the wheel can be seen with permission at Hewish Farm one mile (1·6 km) south of Milton Abbas beside the lane to Milborne St Andrew.

MILL HOUSE WORKING CIDER MUSEUM, OVERMOIGNE
[SY 773871]   **7**

Although not a traditional site, cider is made at this working museum and the best time to visit is from mid-October until December. The interesting collection of cider making equipment has been assembled mostly from outside Dorset, and includes massive wood screw cider presses from Devon of about 1750 vintage. There are mid-nineteenth century portable cider mills from Somerset and a large stone apple crusher with a horse-worked edge runner stone from Gloucestershire. Cider is for sale, and for details, ☎ 0305 852220.

OAKE-WOOD'S BACON FACTORY, GILLINGHAM
[ST 809261]　　　　　　　　　　　　**8**

A brick built factory and office premises close to Gillingham railway station, established in 1847. Oake invented the 'Auto-Cure' method of curing bacon under pressure in cylinders, for which the Danes paid a £4,000 annual royalty. Water was pumped from a well, and extensive cellars beneath the factory were said to be the best in the country for curing–by hanging bacon in the smoke of smouldering hardwoods. 150 were once employed but the factory closed in about 1980. Part of the United Dairies milk and cheese factory remains next door along Station Road. It closed in 1947, becoming a laundry and egg packing station for a few years.

PARK FARM MUSEUM, MILTON ABBAS
[ST 810028]　　　　　　　　　　　　**9**

At the top of the hill above the well known village of Milton Abbas, the thatched cart-horse stables are home for a large collection of Dorset farm implements. There are also old photographs of the village and items from the old brewery. ☎ 0258 880216.

ROKE FARM WHEEL, NEAR BERE REGIS
[SY 835960]　　　　　　　　　　　**10**

Even so high up a chalk valley, there is just enough stream water to turn this low breastshot wheel which stands prominently alongside the lane from Bere Regis to Milborne St Andrew. Dimensions are 22′ × 4′ 2″ (6·7m × 1·27m), and it was designed to power equipment in nearby buildings. It was restored to working order in 1985. The brick building against which it stands has a stone initialled 'SEED' and dated 1880.

TOLLER FRATRUM FARM WHEEL
[SY 578973]　　　　　　　　　　　**11**

A superb wheel sunk almost fully below ground in a building behind the ancient great barn at Toller Fratrum Farm, where one of its last uses was to power sheep shears. This unlikely spot above the main Hooke valley was supplied by water brought in a long leat to a millpond, both now abandoned and dried up, although there is still an iron trough over the lane. The iron overshot wheel remains in good condition, measuring 26′ × 2′ 2″ (7·9m × 0·6m), and a polite request at the farm should gain access to this hidden gem. The hamlet, with its ancient church carvings, is approached from Maiden Newton beneath a low iron bridge of the old Bridport branch railway.

WEST FARM HORSE MILL HOUSE
[SY 840997]　　　　　　　　　　　**12**

This circular wheelhouse is of brick beneath a conical thatched roof, and has been restored in recent years. It once housed a horse gear for driving farm machinery or a cider press. The building stands just south of Winterborne Whitechurch, close to the road to Winterborne Kingston.

Wyke Farm octagonal granary.

WYKE FARM GRANARY
[ST 791267]　　　　　　　　　　　**13**

A small octagonal brick granary and dovecote on staddle stones in the yard of Wyke Farm can be seen from the B3081 as it leaves Gillingham for Wincanton. It is dated to the early nineteenth century.

Roke Farm wheel.

BREWERIES AND MALTINGS

ANSTY BREWERY
[ST 764032]　　　　　　　　　　　　　　**14**

Part of Charles Hall's small rural brewery of 1777 survives as the village hall near the Fox Inn at Lower Ansty. Among his early outlets for beer was the military camp set up outside Weymouth during the French wars. His son Robert took G E I Woodhouse into partnership in 1847, and so the present firm of Hall & Woodhouse had its origins here. Brewing ceased at the turn of the century when the new brewery was completed at Blandford St Mary.

BLANDFORD BREWERY
[ST 886058]　　　　　　　　　　　　　　**15**

This large brewery of Hall & Woodhouse Ltd (Badger Beer) is outside the main town of Blandford Forum, across the Stour in Blandford St Mary. The tall brick brewery and maltings were completed in 1900, when they replaced an earlier brewery which burnt down. The main building contains an original steam engine, built in 1899 by Gimson of Leicester, and once employed for working the mash tuns and hoisting malt sacks. There is a separate administrative block of the period, but the site has been greatly extended in recent years to accommodate lager, soft drinks and canning plants.

CROWN BREWERY, FONTMELL MAGNA
[ST 867169]　　　　　　　　　　　　　　**16**

An excellent example of a small country brewery, rebuilt in its present form in 1876 by George Frederick Applin Flower, whose initials and date are over the door of the handsome brick manager's house on the west side. His sons continued as Flower Bros. under which name the business traded until closure in 1904. The buildings became a depot, and more recently a pottery. A claim to

Crown Brewery,

fame is that the Universal Crown Cork was first used here. The brewery makes an immediate impression on the industrial archaeologist when first seen on the approach from Blandford on the A350 road.

DORCHESTER BREWERY
[SY 692901]　　　　　　　　　　　　　　**17**

The brewery of Eldridge Pope & Co. was built in 1880, to the design of Crickmay of Weymouth. There were direct rail sidings from the London & South Western Railway, and a Dorchester guide-book of the time described the brewery as 'probably the finest pile of buildings devoted to industrial purposes in the south of England'. Indeed, the brewery has notable architecture, with the stylish use of different coloured bricks. There was a serious fire in 1922, but the office block, brewhouse and maltings are substantially as built. Eldridge Pope came here to Weymouth Avenue from the Green Dragon Brewery in Acland Road, which closed in 1883. Charles Eldridge had come here in 1837, the firm becoming Eldridge & Mason in 1850 and eventually Eldridge Pope & Co. in 1871. Among other small breweries in nineteenth century Dorchester, the name of the Pale Ale Brewery can be seen carved over an entrance arch on the north side of High East Street [SY 694908]. This was acquired and rebuilt by the Dragon Brewery in 1854, but closed in 1883. At the corner of Fordington High Street is an old malthouse [SY 696907].

MARNHULL BREWERY
[ST 780182]　　　　　　　　　　　　　　**18**

Thomas Burt started a brewery here at Walton Elm in 1821. Jennings, Jennings & Baker and Styring, White & Co were the later brewers. It was taken over in 1913 by Eldridge Pope, who sold it to Hall & Woodhouse in 1935. The brewery, malthouse and outbuildings were converted for private accommodation, and although the main building has a gable roof its industrial origin is still clear. Just to the east, Hingarston House was the Poplar Elm Brewery of the Andrews family and John Parham before being taken over by Styring, White & Co.

NOTTINGTON MALTHOUSE
[SY 661826]　　　　　　　　　　　　　　**19**

The old malthouse at Nottington near Weymouth was converted to residential accommodation in the 1970s. However, this three-storeyed building retains its distinctive cowl and lucam and is an example of the many rural maltings that operated in mid-nineteenth century Dorset. A date stone is inscribed 'GNS 1834'.

Old Brewery, Bridport.

OLD BREWERY, BRIDPORT
[SY 465921] **20**

The brewery was founded in 1794 and acquired a hundred years later by J C and R H Palmer whose firm still brews here today. Part of the building at the corner of West Bay Road and Skilling Hill Road is thatched, and is said to be the only such brewery in Europe. The buildings are grouped around a yard in the traditional manner and at the rear is an iron waterwheel, measuring 19' × 5' (5·8m × 1·52m) and still capable of raising well water for the brewery. It was built by T Helyear of Bridport in 1879. To the south of the brewhouse is a good slate roofed maltings with typical pyramid-shaped kiln, dated 1859, but not in use as such.

WEYMOUTH BREWERY
[SY 681785] **21**

The most impressive collection of former brewery buildings in Dorset. Brewing ceased in 1986 with the closure of the Devenish Weymouth Brewery in Hope Square. The imposing brick facade of the main brewery is dated 1904. In a window nearby are exhibited two steam engines and a wort pump, used until 1953. The oldest was built by Barrett, Exall & Andrews, of Reading, and may have been shown at Great Exhibition of 1851, while the other engine was built by E S Hindley & Sons of Bourton in about 1890. Both were restored in 1983-85. Alongside the Devenish brewery, on the corner of Hope Square and Spring Road, is the former Hope Brewery of John Groves in red brick. Cooperages, stabling and bottling stores are to the rear of the breweries, while maltings and malt kilns are sited to the east.

WYKE BREWERY, GILLINGHAM
[ST 796266] **22**

This was the brewery of the Matthews family until it was acquired by Hall & Woodhouse in 1963. It closed thereafter but remained as a bottling store for some years. Now converted to flats, the brewery's stone exterior remains largely unchanged beside the B3081, and shows an ambitious architectural style with some Italianate details. The former purpose of the building is clear from the lucam, roof-ridge ventilators and maltkiln. Nearby semi-detached cottages seem to have been built for the brewery workers.

Wyke Brewery.

BRICKWORKS & POTTERIES

BROWNSEA ISLAND
[SZ 013875]   **23**

In the 1850s Colonel Waugh developed a highly mechanised pottery works to produce sewage pipes, sanitary wares and ornamental terra cotta. A horse-worked tramway brought most of the clay from the north side of the island (at Seymours, now on the nature reserve). Waugh had hoped to produce porcelain, but the clay was only suitable for the less profitable coarser ware, and there were soon financial difficulties after so much capital outlay. The works carried on until 1887.

On the south-west coast, around Shard Point, the beach and low cliffs are thick with broken pipes and highly glazed bricks, and there are a few overgrown traces of the works inland. The export pier has been repaired by the National Trust. Nearby can be seen the ruins of Maryland, a model village of sixteen houses in four blocks for the workers.

CHICKERELL
[SY 645798]   **24**

Two chimneys and a continuous kiln are visible beside the B3157 at Chickerell. The associated clay pit under Crook Hill is now partly occupied by a ready-mixed concrete works and depot, and a motor engineering firm. G H Crickmay had a large works here in the 1850s, making bricks, tiles, drain pipes pottery and stoneware. Later owners included Bagg & Sons Ltd and Webb, Major & Co Ltd, before the brickyard closed in 1969.

GODLINGSTON
[SY 020803]   **25**

This is a working brickyard of the Swanage Brick & Tile Co Ltd, where the local clays have been exploited since 1861. There are three oil fired downdraught kilns, each with a capacity of up to 64,000 bricks. The firm specialises in hand-made bricks which have a nationwide market. Although not open to visitors, the works can be seen near Ulwell on the north side of Swanage.

POOLE POTTERY
[SZ 012903]   **26**

The Carters' well known pottery works is still in production on the Quay at Poole. Part dates from the late eighteenth century. The craft showroom has a small museum which contains displays of pottery made here, as well as a reconstructed clay mine and bottle kiln. ☎ 0202 666200.

POWERSTOCK COMMON
[SY 542974]   **27**

The remains of a side fired Suffolk kiln can be seen on part of a woodland nature trail developed by the Dorset Trust for Nature Conservation on Powerstock Common, about 3 miles (5 km) west of Maiden Newton near Bridport. The chamber is 14' 6" (4·4m) long and 12' 3" (3·7m) wide and would have held 20,000 bricks. Under the floor are three arched fire tunnels with unusual cast iron fire doors. It is believed to have been built in 1857 and produced hand-made and perforated wirecut bricks, land drain pipes and some roofing tiles, the raw material being obtained from a clay pit to the south.

VERWOOD POTTERIES
[SU 091077]   **28**

Very little remains of this once widespread industry in the Verwood district. A large kiln mound can be seen on the west side of the B3072 at SU 091077, and this may be the earliest in Verwood. There are two important sites in the vicinity, both on private property. At Potters End [SU 076085], the original potter's house and two buildings survive with a kiln mound–the only eighteenth century group of its type left in the country–and at Sandalholme [SU 079083] survive a kiln mound, a long drying shed and other pottery buildings. This kiln was worked by the Andrews family and closed in about 1907. Beyond Verwood, a kiln mound partially survives at Presseys Corner, Alderholt [SU 122132].

BALL CLAY

BLUE POOL, FURZEBROOK
[SY 935833]   **29**

Blue Pool is just south of Furzebrook, which is the main processing centre for the Purbeck clay industry. It is a strange place for an industrial monument, but this popular beauty spot is a flooded clay pit surrounded by trees. Minute clay particles in the water diffract sunlight, giving varying shades of deep blue or green under the right conditions. The small museum at the site has a display on the history of the ball clay and pottery industries, and exhibits include a *tubal*, the curious narrow spade once used for cutting clay. ☎ 09295 51408.

Blue Pool is just one of many flooded clay pits in the area, but is the best known and most accessible. Modern clay pits and mines are generally well hidden, but for example, the covered storage bins and inclined shaft of Norden Mine [SY 949827] can be seen from a footpath. The museum at the Poole Pottery (site 26) has a reconstructed clay mine.

Suckthumb Quarry.   *P. Trim*

STONE QUARRYING

BILL QUARRIES, PORTLAND
[SY 676684]   **30**

The very tip of Portland is low with little overburden, making quarrying easy although the quality of the stone is not as good as elsewhere. The famous Pulpit Rock was created by removing a natural arch in about 1875. There are small working faces, piles of scappled blocks and waste rock. The course of a tramway with stone sleeper blocks passes south of the lighthouse to a low cliff where barges were loaded [SY 6806850]. The present crane here is not the original and is used for hoisting and lowering fishing boats. There are other cranes and small quarries further along the coast to the northeast. The first is Cave Hole Quarry [SY 696691] where a timber derrick is positioned above a wide cave opening, with the quarry a little way inland. At Longstone Ope [SY 687692] are two cranes now used for lowering fishing boats, and scappled blocks piled up but never shipped. The quarry openings are much deeper than on the Bill, and some faces show where they have been cut by channelling machines.

DANCING LEDGE QUARRY, PURBECK
[SY 997769]   **31**

A popular spot where gently sloping stone ledges give access to the sea. On the main sea-washed ledge can be seen the tracks used by horn-carts for carrying stone for loading into waiting barges. The main quarry is above, with some underground workings behind. It was last worked in 1914. Hedbury is the next cliff quarry westwards towards Seacombe.

EAST WEARE, PORTLAND
[SY 703715]   **32**

A great landslipped area of tumbled blocks which were among the first to be worked for export from King's, Folly and Durdle Piers. Wren's original workings were here. Much of East Weare is in Ministry of Defence property, but Penn's Weare can be approached from Church Ope Cove.

LANGTON MATRAVERS MUSEUM, PURBECK
[SY 998789]   **33**

Just behind the church, the Coach House Museum is devoted to the Purbeck stone industry and well worth a visit. It contains many items and photographs of the Purbeck stone industry, including a reconstructed stone 'mine' of the sort once common in the surrounding district. ☎ 0929 423168.

MARNHULL QUARRIES
[ST 796198]   **34**

Much of the land to the east of Marnhull has been quarried for a freestone which made a good local building stone (such as in the fine church) as well as being burnt for lime. Cottages can be seen in old sunken quarries at Salisbury Street [ST 786188], but the most extensive area is on both sides of the B3092 at Gannetts, where one part is still worked in a small way [ST 796198].

PORTESHAM QUARRIES
[SY 610859]   **35**

Limestone quarries on the hillside to the east of the village were connected by an incline from the Abbotsbury railway in 1887. William Manfield leased these quarries and gravel pits further up the hill near Hardy's Monument, but by 1895 there were no workers recorded and thereafter only two or three. Intermittent working appears to have ceased in 1928. There were two limekilns, but only part of one remains. The course of the incline can be barely traced, but part of a protruding rail is a clue.

PURBECK MARBLE WORKINGS
[SY 984796]   **36**

Overgrown medieval pits along the thin seam of Purbeck marble can be traced at the foot of the limestone escarpment which extends from Peveril Point to Warbarrow Tout. Some, for example, can be seen from the lane between Harman's Cross and Sunnydown, near Downshay Farm.

ST ALDHELM'S QUARRY, PURBECK
[SY 965761]   **37**

This is a working quarry and the only one in the district where the Purbeck-Portland stone is extracted for masonry. W J Haysom & Son have installed a modern stone dressing plant, but the quarry retains the last complete timber derrick standing in a Purbeck or, indeed, any Dorset quarry. The cliff top of St Aldhelm's Head [SY 962754] has been quarried in the past, leaving some striking pinnacles.

SEACOMBE QUARRY, PURBECK
[SY 984766]   **38**

Where the dry valley of Seacombe Bottom meets the coast there were quarries for the Purbeck-Portland stone, at work from about 1700 until the 1930s. There are underground workings with the roof supported by uncut pillars and precarious piles of blocks. By 1839, uses of stone from this quarry had been for the clock house on Dover pier, Winchester prison, West India Docks, lighthouses at Margate and the Isle of Wight, and numerous churches and bridges in the county.

SUCKTHUMB QUARRY, PORTLAND
[SY 687707]   **39**

Contains the only standing timber derrick in a Portland quarry, a 3 ton crane without a jib. The quarry clearly shows the method of working, with a deep gully and bench behind. A large area has been quarried and the Coombefield and Weston sections have been worked in recent years.

A quarry mouth.

Seacombe Quarry.

TILLY WHIM QUARRY, PURBECK
[SZ 031769]   **40**

Purbeck-Portland beds were worked underground and the stone loaded into barges from the cliff. Tilly is believed to have been the quarry owner's name, while 'whim' refers to the crane used for lowering the stone. John Mowlem is said to have worked here as a boy before the quarry closed in about 1814. George Burt opened these man-made caves as an attraction for the public, but they were closed when the rock became unsafe ninety years later. They remain visible from the coastal footpath above, and from the west.

TOUT QUARRY, PORTLAND
[SY 685727]   **41**

An interesting quarry almost at the top of the island, from where much stone waste was tipped over the West Cliff. Within the quarry stone sleeper blocks record the course of branches from the Merchants' Railway. Possibly the finest monument on all Portland is a beautifully constructed drystone arch, with a keystone inscribed 'J. C. Lano 1854'. Lano was the manager of the quarry. A second Lano arch of 1862 was for a tramway beneath the Weston road into the Independent Quarries. A walk along the top of West Cliff reveals how much waste stone was tipped over the edge. Towards the Trade Quarries there are several stone buttresses which carried the tipping tramways across the clifftop track [SY 683723].

WINSPIT QUARRY, PURBECK
[SY 977761]   **42**

Extensive cliffside quarries and underground workings are found below Worth Matravers at the end of a dry valley flanked by superb strip lynchets. Stone was quarried here from the eighteenth century down until 1945.

OTHER MINERAL WORKINGS

HENGISTBURY HEAD IRONSTONE
[SZ 176906]   **43**

Ironstone occurs in the sandy beds on this headland at the mouth of Christchurch harbour. It was quarried in 1848-70 by the Welsh-based Hengistbury Head Mining Co., managed by J E Holloway, a Southampton coal merchant. The ironstone was taken in barges to Southampton, where it was transferred as ballast for coal ships returning empty to South Wales. At first large ironstone blocks, or doggers, were collected from the foreshore, but this soon led to erosion of the soft cliffs which they had protected. The most visible feature today is a weathered opencast working which almost cuts the headland in two. Holloway's Dock was cut for the barges which came to load. Another ironstone quarry was the Batters on the north side, since dammed to make a pond.

KIMMERIDGE SHALE
[SY 909788]   **44**

A site with a long industrial history, with evidence of organised production of shale products in the iron age. Sometimes called Kimmeridge Coal, the bituminous shale was quarried along the cliffs for use as a fuel by local inhabitants. In the nineteenth century there were various attempts to produce gas and oil commercially. Wanostrocht & Co. had a plant at Wareham producing gas for lamps in 1848, and ten years later won a contract to light the streets of Paris with gas made from Kimmeridge shale. Oil and fertilizer were also produced. The works was taken over in 1862 by the Wareham Oil & Candle Co. and other firms followed. For a while sanitary carbon was produced to filter sewage. The last major working was in 1883-90 by the Kimmeridge Oil & Carbon Co., who built a tramway inland from a pier. The shale was worked underground, notably at the Manfield Pit [SY 917783]. A walk eastwards along the shore reveals old levels in the cliff face with the occasional tramway rail protruding. Cement stone was also worked here. Industrial activity at Kimmeridge included an alum works, salt works and glasshouse in the early seventeenth century.

Abbot's limekiln.

LIMEKILNS

BISHOP'S, ABBOTSBURY
[SY 587858]   **45**

A small limekiln, about a century old and partly restored by the County Council. An illustrated information board explains the limeburning process. Here at the Bishop's Limekiln Picnic Site there is a good viewpoint beside a lane which climbs steeply north-east above Abbotsbury village.

CHURCH KNOWLE
[SY 945822]   **46**

An interesting limekiln at the foot of Knowle Hill, with a small chalk quarry behind. It is unusual in having a small limeburner's 'bothy' built into the west side. It has been restored by the Dorset Countryside Volunteers.

LANGTON HERRING   **47**

[SY 622825] A most unusual limekiln standing alone in a sloping field below the lane from Langton Cross into the village. A broad arch gains access to the drawhole which is below ground level on the lower side.

LIMEKILN HILL, WEST BEXINGTON
[SY 538871]   **48**

Just visible from the B3157 coast road, this limekiln lies at the lower edge of a small overgrown lime-stone quarry. It is in good condition and has an inverted V arch to the draw hole. A spring emerging from the back of the kiln must have caused problems and makes an unusual feature. The hillside site is owned by the National Trust and overlooks West Bexington. The Dorset coastal footpath passes close by.

PORTLAND
[SY 691727]   **49**

A limekiln on the east side of the main road to Easton, difficult to spot as a low building surrounds the drawhole arch.

SHILLINGSTONE
[ST 823098]   **50**

A working chalk quarry and limeworks, cut into the wooded escarpment of Shillingstone Hill and clearly visible from many miles away. Two pairs of kilns have been burning continuously since the 1930s. The Shillingstone Lime & Stone Co Ltd. was established in 1924 and is now the last producer in Dorset, sending hydrated lime to builders' merchants as far as Gloucester and Cornwall. A grinder at the mouth of the kilns is by the Patent Lightning Crusher Co Ltd, and is said to be the oldest such working in England. The chalk quarry has an old aerial ropeway system installed during the Second World War.

FOUNDRIES & ENGINEERING WORKS

BOURTON FOUNDRY
[ST 775310]   **51**

There was an important foundry in Bourton, where at one time a quarter of the village was employed. Most of the site is now a milk factory. Daniel Maggs' foundry was established in the mid-nineteenth century at a former corn mill and flax mill, and was later worked by Maggs & Hindley and then E S Hindley & Son. Suitable moulding sand was available nearby. Edge tools, agricultural machinery, and portable and stationary steam engines were all built. After 1906, steam wagons were supplied too. Hindley patented a high speed engine which could drive electrical generators. For such a small village far from any major centre this was quite an achievement, and the foundry sported a 60' x 2' (18·3m x 0·6m) waterwheel which was built in 1837. It was dismantled in 1918, but the wheelpit remains and the mark of the great wheel can be seen on a pillar which supported the launder. Some foundry buildings and a large mill-pond also survive, and there are contoured leats in the grounds of Bullpits house, where permission to visit may be sought.

Waterwheels were supplied to various mills including Cann, Melbury Abbas, Stour Provost and one for pumping water just across the border in Wiltshire at Stourhead Gardens. A recently renovated water trough near Shaftesbury is another example of their work. Gillingham Museum has a cast iron plate from Lodden Bridge, inscribed 'E. S. Hindley, Bourton, 1868'. A Hindley steam engine is displayed at the Weymouth Brewery (site 21), while another from the Sherborne gas works is in the local museum.

LOTT & WALNE FOUNDRY, DORCHESTER
[SY 696907]   **52**

The premises of Lott & Walne Ltd at Fordington High Street were vacated in early 1988, although iron founding ceased many years before. The main brick building probably dates from the first half of the nineteenth century and has a crane overhanging the street, but unfortunately the works bell on the roof has disappeared. While also acting as agents for other firms, Lott & Walne made their own agricultural machinery. Parts were cast for water wheels, and the firm made water carts a speciality, selling them all over the country. Notable products which can be seen around Dorchester include a superb clock tower in Borough Gardens, drain covers, and a very stout lamp post outside the off-licence of the Dorchester Brewery in Weymouth Avenue. There is a collection of wooden patterns dating from 1875 to 1932 in the Dorset County Museum, which itself has an interesting piece of Victorian iron work in its structure.

DAW'S WHEELWRIGHT & ENGINEERING SHOP, SOUTH PERROTT
[ST 474068]   **53**

A complete wheelwright, engineering and blacksmith shop, belonging to Mr Ellis Daw who worked here all his life. Power for belt driven lathes and saws is supplied by a Petters engine installed brand new in 1919. Carts and wagons were once made and repaired here and the site also includes a paint shop and a saw pit. The site, at the rear of Winton Cottage on the A356, can be visited by appointment (☎: Corscombe 234). It can be seen at work on the first Sunday of August during the village festival week.

Improved iron water cart — manufactured by the Lott & Walne Foundry of Dorchester.

MILLS

ALDERHOLT MILL
[SU 119143]   **54**

In a pleasant setting on Ashford Water, right on the border with Hampshire and just west of Fordingbridge. There was a mill here in the fourteenth century, but the present mill is much later. It worked until 1942, and has been under restoration since 1982 when it became a craft shop and art gallery. The machinery is once again in working order and flour can be produced. The iron undershot wheel measures 11' x 7' 10" (3·3m x 2·6m), and was made by William Munden of Ringwood. ☎ 0425 53130.

CANN MILL, NEAR SHAFTESBURY
[ST 872208]   **55**

A working mill where N R Stoate & Sons Ltd produce wholemeal flour. The building was rebuilt after a fire in 1954. An unusual windmill on the mill's flat roof and a large millpond make this a conspicuous landmark from A350 just south of Shaftesbury. The watermill has an overshot wheel by Hindley of Bourton. The windmill was built in 1971 and is not just a curiosity, for it does work from time to time. Cann and Melbury Abbas are the only survivors of five watermills on just a mile stretch of the River Sturkel. Of the others, French Mill is now a house.

FIDDLEFORD MILL
[ST 801136]   **56**

There is a medieval house here with a fine timber roof, and open to the public (English Heritage). However, the mill is a small stone building to the north on what must be a long established site. On the mill wall is an interesting inscription of 1566, which reads:

> Operam dedi 1566 meis sump'salien sis
> He thatt wyll have here anythinge done
> Let him com fryndley he shall be welcom
> A frynd to the owner and enemy to no man
> Pass al here freely to whom they can
> For the tale of trothe I do alway professe
> Myller be true disgrace not thy vest
> If falsehead appeere the faulte shall be thyne
> And if sharpe punishment think me not unkind
> Therefore be true ye shal thee behove
> To please God chiefly that liveth above.

The waterwheel was replaced by an Armfield turbine to work two pairs of stones, but the mill is now disused. This is a pleasant spot on the Stour just downstream from Sturminster Mill.

Upwey Mill.

KINGS MILL, MARNHULL
[ST 766172]   **57**

A substantial stone mill building on the Stour, highly visible from Kings Mill Bridge on the road from Marnhull to Stalbridge. Little remains of the wheel.

LITTON CHENEY MILL
[SY 550904]   **58**

The mill has been converted to a house, but the large wheel (built in 1866 by Coombs of Beaminster) can be seen; dimensions, 11' 6" x 6' 6" (3·5m x 2m). The mill race joins the stream which runs down the side of the village street.

MAIDEN NEWTON MILL
[SY 596977]   **59**

There were two undershot waterwheels here until the present large iron wheel was installed, measuring 15' x 12' (4·6m x 3·6m) and made by Winter & Hossey of Dorchester. The mill has been a carpet factory but is now a small engineering works. It can be seen from the A356 as it crosses the River Frome in Maiden Newton. The nearby Forge Cottage has an iron wheel bonding plate set in the ground outside.

MANGERTON MILL, NEAR BRIDPORT
[SY 490957]   **60**

A pair of wheels, each 12' x 4' (3·6m x 1·2m), drove a grist mill on one side and a flax mill on the other. Originally breastshot, they were later rolled out and reversed to become overshot. The flax mill became a saw mill, and its wheel was replaced by a turbine which can be seen still in place. The corn mill has been restored to working order and is open to the public. There is also a tea room here. ☎ 030 885 224.

MELBURY ABBAS MILL, NEAR SHAFTESBURY

[ST 877207]   **61**

A mill in working order and open to the public. At the south end of the range is a fine overshot wheel, fed from the millpond immediately behind. It was built in 1875 by E S Hindley of Bourton, and measures 11′ x 5′ 6″ (3·3m x 1·7m). Refurbished in March 1985, it now works two pairs of Derbyshire millstones for animal feed and some flour. A Countryside Museum includes cider making equipment, farming implements, vintage cars and motor cycles. ☎ 0747 2163.

PLACE MILL, CHRISTCHURCH

[SZ 160924]   **62**

This small mill belonged to Christchurch Priory until the Dissolution in 1539, and continued working until the early twentieth century. It has been restored and is open to the public during the summer. There is an attractive walk beside the millstream from the Town Bridge on the Avon.

PORTLAND WINDMILLS

[SY 690713 & 691712]   **63**

Two stone windmill towers at Cottonfields [SY 690713] and Top Growlands [SY 691712] are the only visible remains of thirty known windmills in Dorset. They may date back to the 1600s, when mills were first recorded here, and worked until the 1890s.

STURMINSTER NEWTON MILL

[ST 782135]   **64**

At the weir on the Stour near Sturminster Bridge, this is a working and demonstration mill, restored in 1981. It was in two parts, with the earlier stone building possibly of the sixteenth century, while the northern brick built mill is eighteenth century. Between them were two undershot wheels, the last ones dating from 1849 and supplied by William Munden of Ringwood. In 1904 the wheels were replaced by a 'British Empire' turbine made by Joseph J Armfield who was Munden's successor. Although more efficient, turbines lack the excitement of a turning wheel. However, the milling machinery can be seen at work producing animal feeds and flour for sale. ☎ 0258 73151. The next mill upstream is Cutt Mill [ST 776165], a picturesque spot at a weir and footbridge near Hinton St Mary. Although the wooden undershot wheel is broken, the machinery survives intact inside the brick and stone mill building.

SUTTON POYNTZ MILL

[SY 706837]   **65**

A distinctive brick mill building, partly converted to living accommodation. The wheel has gone, but the millpond is a picturesque feature behind. The miller's house is of stone, like much of the rest of the village.

THROOP MILL, NEAR BOURNEMOUTH

[SZ 113958]   **66**

Throop Mill survives in good condition at a long weir on the Stour to the north of Bournemouth. Of the six sluice gates, three are by the Dorset Ironfoundry Co of Poole. Three others are by Lott & Walne of Dorchester and inscribed 'Avon Stour Catchment Board, 1936'.

Throop Mill and weir.

UPWEY MILL, NEAR WEYMOUTH

[SY 663851]   **67**

A fine working mill building with four floors, and dating from 1802. The huge waterwheel measures 22′ x 9′ (6·7m x 2·7m) and is set within the building at the north end. It is fed by two streams so that it is both overshot and breast shot, and drives two pairs of stones although there is evidence that there were five pairs at one time. The mill is in Church Street, and visitors are welcome. ☎ 0305 814233.

WALFORD MILL, WIMBORNE

[SU 009007]   **68**

The brick mill building, in Knobcrook Road, was restored and converted in 1986 to become the Walford Mill Craft Centre of the Dorset Craft Guild (☎ 0202 841400). The old mill cottage is now a gallery, while the interior of the mill itself has workshop space for craftsmen and a craft school on the top floor. The mill dates from about 1686, although it was much rebuilt in the early nineteenth century. The mountings for two undershot waterwheels can be seen inside the building. There was a steam engine, of which the stack survives, and in later years a diesel engine provided power. A single millstone outside is a clue to the building's origins. The Walford water pumping station (site 144) can be seen from the riverside walk.

Walford Mill.

WEST MILL, BRIDPORT
[SY 463931]   **69**

A striking brick building with cast iron window frames beside West Street, now converted to an architect's office. It was built in 1878 on the site of a corn and balling mill of which the north wing remains. A turbine by Hick Hargreaves of Bolton was installed in 1886. Water from sluices can be seen passing beneath the building.

WHITE MILL, NEAR STURMINSTER MARSHALL
[ST 958006]   **70**

This large brick mill dates from the eighteenth century and ceased work in 1944. The water-wheel has gone, but the wooden gear survives and is said to be the oldest in the county. The mill and attached miller's house stand near the picturesque Whitemill Bridge across the Stour. White Mill is owned by the National Trust and restoration is in progress.

TEXTILES, ROPES & NETS

BOURTON CLOTH MILLS
[ST 775312]   **71**

Bullpits is only recognisable as a house, but was built around a cloth or flax mill of the early eighteenth century. Flax was grown in the nearby fields, while on the slope below the house three leats were used for flax retting as well as serving Maggs & Hindley's foundry (site 52). One has been fully restored. The Maggs family manufactured sacks alongside the foundry, employing over 200 in the mid-nineteenth century. A second cloth mill of 1820 was behind the premises of the Bourton Fencing Co, beside the main road through this north Dorset village [ST 777309].

BRIDPORT MUSEUM
[SY 466929]   **72**

The museum and art gallery in South Street has a good collection of rope and net making machinery preserved here at the heart of the industry. Items include a rope making jack and a 'jumper' loom, in use for net making at Bridport from 1840 until 1968. There are also photographs of the industry. ☎ 0308 22116.

BURTON MILL, BURTON BRADSTOCK
[SY 490897]   **73**

Beside the River Bride, this stone built mill has lost its wheel and has been converted to residential use. The sluice, by Lotte & Walne, remains. On a low range facing Grove Road is an inscription recording the mill's significance. It reads: 'This flax-swingling mill, the first introduced into the West of England, was erected by Richard Roberts, 1803.' Roberts did much to transform the local flax indus-try from a craft to factory basis, and he also oper-ated Grove Mill in the village.

COURT WORKS, BRIDPORT
[SY 464931]   **74**

Now the centre of the modern industry of Brid-port-Gundry Ltd., this site retains some nineteenth century features. The office block on West Street is dated 1844 and some older buildings to the rear are the survivors of a serious fire in 1949. One brick warehouse has a date stone 'G.PERRIMAN 1811'.

GROVE MILL, BURTON BRADSTOCK
[SY 488894]   **75**

Off Mill Street, this was the second site operated by Richard Roberts in Burton Bradstock. It was a single storeyed factory, later steam powered. A terrace of workers' cottages beneath the church-yard wall has a date stone inscribed 'R R 1800'.

NORTH MILLS, BRIDPORT
[SY 465935]   **76**

The former works of William Hounsell & Co., and now an industrial estate. There were two power-ful steam engines and a waterwheel working at this complex, which produced lines, twines and nets. Despite demolition, much survives, including hemp stores, walks and the old tar house.

PRIORY MILLS, BRIDPORT
[SY 463927]   **77**

Built in the 1830s for Stephen Whetham & Sons, makers of lines, twines and canvas. It was steam powered and the location of the beam engine can be identified by the large round-headed window in the mill building. Whetham's former warehouse is nearby, a tall stone building at the corner of Rope Walks and Gundry Lane [SY 465928].

PYMORE MILLS AND VILLAGE
[SY 470946]   **78**

The former works and community of the Pymore Mill Co which manufactured flax and hemp. The flax mill was converted from a linseed oil, grist and balling mill by 1812. It became a factory but has remained a ruin since it burnt down in 1959. The complex is best viewed as a whole, and includes later mills (now a furniture manufactory), millpond, sluices, ropewalk, manager's house, office, school, apprentices' and workers' houses. This fascinating site is awaiting restoration.

ST MICHAEL'S TRADING ESTATE, BRIDPORT
[SY 463928]   **79**

The former premises of Bridport Industries Ltd., on the west side of St Michael's Lane. This extensive site was transformed in the late nineteenth and early twentieth centuries. From south to north were the St Michael's Works of William Edwards, formerly a bleaching ground, the Stover Works of W S Edwards, and the works of William Gale. A notable feature is a low red brick building with a square tower.

SHERBORNE SILK MILL
[ST 635159]   **80**

The original silk mill was at Westbury Mill of about 1753, which is now incorporated in the Marglass factory which makes synthetic textiles. Over the road, at the junction of Westbury and Ottery Lane, is a conspicuous mill range erected by the Willmotts in 1840. Across the playing fields to the north, is a long terrace of workers' houses.

YARN BARTON, BEAMINSTER
[ST 481014]   **81**

A sailcloth and netting factory, now disused. It is a low building of two storeys alongside the car park entrance off Fleet Street. The earliest part dates from 1780. Another sailcloth factory at Beaminster was Whatley Mill, now converted to a house.

ROADS

BAGBER BRIDGE
[ST 764156]   **82**

An iron bridge over the River Lydden, supplied by the Coalbrookdale Co. The engineer was W Dawes. The cast iron girders were strengthened with wrought iron rods, and despite modern work the bridge retains its original appearance with a gentle arch and hand rails.

BARNES CROSS PILLAR BOX, HOLWELL
[ST 693117]   **83**

A pillar box, made by John Butt of Gloucester in 1853, and the oldest still in use in England. It features a vertical letter slot with weather flap. It is at a lonely spot on the fringe of the Blackmoor Vale, and the approach from Bishop's Caundle crosses the interesting Cornford Bridge [ST 692120], a narrow structure of 1480 but much repaired in the eighteenth century.

Post box (1853) at Barnes Cross.

BLANDFORD FORUM MILESTONE
[ST 883061]   **84**

This milestone in West Street gives the distance to Hyde Park Corner (104 miles). There is another, for example, on the A351 one mile (1·6 km) from Wareham [SY 924889].

BOURNEMOUTH TRANSPORT MUSEUM
[SZ 109944]   **85**

A large collection of public transport vehicles from the Bournemouth district, including a 1901 tramcar body, a restored 1914 tram, trolleybuses, and motor buses from 1910 to 1969. The museum is at the bus depot in Mallard Road and opening is restricted. ☎ 0202 21009.

CHALBURY MILEPOST
[SU 011075]   **86**

A cast iron milepost giving the distances of 5 miles (8 km) to Wimborne and Cranborne and the name 'Poole Trust'. There are several of these between Wimborne and Cranborne. There is a prominent example of this type where the A351 Wareham road leaves the roundabout at Lytchett Minster [SY 955925].

CHARMINSTER MILESTONE
[SY 671919]   **87**

A tall milestone beside the A37 just west of Charminster has an iron plate which reads '2 Dorchester by the New Road/Maiden Newton 6'. The 'New road' refers to an early example of a by-pass which avoided Charminster village. An Act of 1840 authorised this for the Maiden Newton Trust.

CHARMINSTER TOLLHOUSE
[SY675921]   **88**

A fine example of a small tollhouse, six-sided under a slate roof, beside the A37 just north-west of Dorchester. It is on the 'New Road' by-passing Charminster.

COSMORE TURNPIKE STONE
[ST 676056]   **89**

A small stone with an iron plate inscribed 'Here ends the Weymouth and Dorchester Trust', at the foot of the chalk escarpment on the high road from Dorchester to Sherborne. The milestones on this route have shaped iron plates and the first up the hill [ST 673043] is exactly 9 miles (14·4 km) between each town.

ENMORE GREEN WATER TROUGH, NEAR SHAFTESBURY
[ST 859234]   **90**

An iron water trough, by Maggs & Hindley of Bourton, with a lion water spout set in a greensand wall, with the date 1844 carved above. This must have been a welcome spot in the days of horse transport, being part way up the long hill from Gillingham into Shaftesbury (now B3081). It was restored in 1988.

FIFEHEAD NEVILLE PACKHORSE BRIDGE
[ST 772111]   **91**

A small restored packhorse bridge beside a ford across the River Divelish. Two pointed arches carry the footway, with a single cutwater on the

upstream side. Timber handrails have been added in more recent times.

HORN HILL TUNNEL, BEAMINSTER
[ST 467032]   **92**

The A3066 passes though this tunnel which was built in ten months in 1831-2. It is 345' (105m) long and was originally lit by paraffin lamps. It is not easy to stop and read the inscriptions of the portals which proclaim that Giles Russell of Beaminster was responsible.

Horn Hill Tunnel.

LONGMOOR MILEPOST, NEAR GILLINGHAM
[ST 828290]   **93**

A cast iron plate of the Wincanton Trust between Mere and Shaftesbury, at a cross roads 2 miles (3·2 km) north-east of Gillingham, gives 'Shaftesbury 5 Mere 2'. The smaller words 'Town Hall' (referring to Shaftesbury) have been painted out. It is the only milepost on this road which passes through Motcombe village.

MOTCOMBE TURNPIKE COTTAGE
[ST 835243]   **94**

A tollhouse on the B3081 Shaftesbury-Gillingham at a junction to Motcombe. It is a substantial house in local greensand, with a datestone of 1866. Milestones on the Gillingham road have shield shaped iron plates giving the details. The parish is carved on the edge of the stones.

OBORNE TOLLHOUSE, SHERBORNE
[ST 651177]   **95**

A single storey tollhouse beside the A30, a mile outside Sherborne. It is lower than the road, suggesting how the highway has been built up over the years since it was built. The nearby cast iron milepost and one at 2 miles (3·6 km) from Sher borne are rectangular with a cap. There is a good two storey tollhouse beyond Oborne at White Post on the B3145 [ST 640193].

SHAFTESBURY MILEPOST
[ST 866228] **96**

A cast iron milepost giving the distances 'Sherborn 15 Salisbury 20' on two faces, and the parish St Peters Shaftesbury' down the centre. It was cast by Cockey of Frome. The next towards Sherborne, in 'Motcomb' parish [ST 852233], also gives 15 miles to Sherborne! This type of the Shaftesbury & Sherborne Trust extends along the A30 to beyond West Stour [ST 762218] and 4 miles (6·4 km) eastwards into Wiltshire at Donhead St Andrew.

STURMINSTER NEWTON BRIDGE
[ST784135] **97**

A fifteenth century bridge across the Stour, rebuilt in 1820. The datestone for this is upside down at the base of the central cutwater, which enables it to be read from above. There is a 'transportation' plate here. An arched causeway keeps the road above flood level on north side.

TARRANT HINTON TOLLHOUSE
[ST 948114] **98**

Beside the A354 Salisbury to Blandford road, the route of the Harnham, Blandford & Dorchester Trust. An L-shaped single storey tollhouse with iron 'gothic' windows beneath a slate roof. Inscribed on a wall are the date and letters '1827 PD - TG'. A nearby milestone is incised 'Blandford 5 Sarum 17', the latter being the old name for Salisbury.

THISTLE HILL TUNNEL, CHARMOUTH
[SY 348948] **99**

The main A35 passes through this tunnel at the top of the climb west of Charmouth. Built at the same time as the Horn Hill tunnel in 1832, it is only 220 feet (67m) long.

THROOP ROAD GAS LAMP POSTS, BOURNEMOUTH
[SZ 109961] **100**

Attractively decorated cast-iron lamp posts are a nostalgic feature as they are still in use for gas lights. The road passes Throop Mill and weir.

TUCKTON BRIDGE, CHRISTCHURCH
[SZ 149923] **101**

An earlier timber bridge of 1883 was replaced by this iron and concrete one in 1905, so that the Bournemouth trams could cross the Stour from Southbourne to Christchurch. It was a tollbridge

until 1943, by which time the trams had been replaced by trolley buses.

TYNEHAM TELEPHONE KIOSK
[SY 882803] **102**

Tyneham village is best known for its evacuation for military training during the Second World War. It still remains empty within the ranges, but there is public access when there is no live firing. Rather oddly, outside a row of roofless cottages is a rare telephone box of concrete and wood with an ornate roof. This is the 'Kiosk No. 1', a design introduced in 1921. It is much different from the more familiar Kiosk No.6, which was designed by Sir Giles Gilbert Scott and produced in the Silver Jubilee year of King George V.

WHITEMILL BRIDGE, STURMINSTER MARSHALL
[ST 958005] **103**

On the Stour at Whitemill. A narrow eight arched bridge, with cutwaters and refuges on each pier, using mainly heathstone, with limestone and some greensand. It may have been built in 1175, on the old road west from Wimborne, but lost its traffic when Julian Bridge [SZ 0049990] was built downstream. Crawford Bridge [ST 919020] is the next one upstream and dates from about 1530. It has a marked hump in the centre and was widened on the downstream side in 1719.

WOOL OLD BRIDGE
[SY 845872] **104**

On the Frome beside the manor house made famous in Thomas Hardy's *Tess of the d'Urbervilles*. It is probably fifteenth century, but was repaired in 1607 and two centuries later. Stonework includes dark brown heathstone.

WEST ALLINGTON TOLLHOUSE, BRIDPORT
[SY 457930] **105**

A large tollhouse in brick, with overhanging slate roof. This was at the West Gate of the Bridport First District Trust.

COUNTY COUNCIL OF DORSET
NOTICE TO DRIVERS OF WAGGONS
AND OTHER HEAVY VEHICLES
— TAKE NOTICE —
THAT THE COUNTY COUNCIL WILL
PROSECUTE ANY PERSON CAUSING
INJURY TO THE SURFACE OF THIS
MAIN ROAD BY THE IMPROPER USE
OF A SKIDPAN DRAGSHOE OR
OTHERWISE
BY ORDER
DORSET COUNTY COUNCIL

RAILWAYS FOR INDUSTRY

KIMMERIDGE TRAMWAYS, PURBECK

106

An Act of 1847 permitted the building of the first tramway, which was worked in 1848-54 by the Bituminous Shale Co. There are slight traces where it runs behind Clavell Tower and Hen Cliff, with a cutting descending towards the quay [SY 910787]. The second tramway was more ambitious, worked in 1883-90 by the Kimmeridge Oil & Carbon Co., curving around inland for nearly a mile (1·6 km) across the fields from a pier to the Manfield Shaft [SY 917783].

FAYLE'S TRAMWAY, PURBECK

107

This was the first railway in Dorset, built by Benjamin Fayle in 1806-7. It was a plateway, 3½ miles (5·6km) long, to carry ball clay from Fayle's works at Norden to Middlebere Quay on Poole Harbour. It was of 3' 9" (1·14m) gauge, with 3' (0·9m) long tramway plates. Stone sleeper blocks survive in isolated sections across the heaths. There are also some cuttings and embankments.

Two short tunnels were built under the Wareham-Corfe road near Norden at SY 948832. A section of the old A351 survives as a lane and footpath after road improvements in 1988, and the two tunnels can be seen here, their old trackways in flooded gullies. The dressed keystone of the north tunnel is inscribed 'BF 1807', making this one of the earliest railway tunnels in the country. A

Fayles Tramway Tunnel

third tunnel was built under the Studland road [SY 963827] in about 1850. The course of the tramway crosses Slepe Lane, between Corfe and Arne, at SY 963853. On one side the track serves Middlebere Farm, but the other traverses the lonely

Hartland Moor nature reserve and can be followed on foot, with gentle curves passing through a cutting and over a low embankment.

Middlebere Quay [SY 975866] has lain abandoned since 1905 when the tramway was replaced by the Goathorn Tramway to Goathorn Pier [SZ 016863], a wooden jetty on South Deep, less silted, and serving claypits at Newton. This lasted until about 1936. In 1948 a small section of the tramway was relaid to 1' 11½" (0·6m) gauge around Norden where there was a depot and exchange sidings with the Swanage railway. Small diesels were used and the last steam locomotive, the *Russell*, has been preserved in North Wales.

PIKE TRAMWAY, PURBECK

108

Built by Pike Bros. in 1838-40 to link their clay pits and mines around Furzebrook with Ridge Wharf on the tidal River Frome near Wareham. Originally a horse tramway of 2' 8" (0·8m) gauge, steam locomotives were introduced after 1866 and named with Latin numbers from *Primus* to *Septimus*. *Secundus*, dating from 1874, is now preserved in the Birmingham Museum of Science and Industry. There was a works at Ridge, but Furzebrook was the headquarters of the system, and an engine shed survives today amid the modern processing works. To the south-west are numerous overgrown branches, while the track to Ridge Wharf is a straight line due north. A bump in the Arne road at SY 937863 shows where it crossed and a section of rail is still in position. Ridge Wharf is now a boat yard.

MERCHANTS' RAILWAY, PORTLAND

109

To cater for the great increase in stone traffic and relieve the burden on horses, the 4' 6" (1·37m) gauge Merchants' Railway was built in 1826 from the top of Portland. Here, there were branches into Tout Quarry, and trucks were loaded by crane at Priory Corner. Two lines, with stone sleeper blocks in place, can be seen curving around the west flank of the Verne to the top of the the Freemans Incline at SY 689738. From here, stone laden trucks descended to Castleton Pier on Portland harbour. A complex of bridges and inclines at SY 692733 is of a later date and is associated with the Portland Breakwater works, but connected with the Merchant's Railway. On the north-east side of Portland was the Admiralty or Breakwater Railway of 1847, an incline with three winding drums at intervals. It descended from the Admiralty and Convict quarries to the start of the breakwater, and is now in Ministry of Defence property. The Merchants' Railway closed in 1939.

SWANAGE PIER RAILWAY, PURBECK
[SZ 033787] 110

Narrow gauge rails can be seen along the Quay. This tramway was built in 1859 at the same time as the pier, to connect it with the stone bankers and quarries at Swanage and Langton Matravers. There were to be branches and an inclined plane, but it was only built as far as Commercial Road. John Mowlem and George Burt were among the first directors.

RAILWAYS

BINCOMBE TUNNEL
[SY 673855] 111

A classic tunnel 814 yards (744m) long takes the GWR beneath Bincombe Down, the high ridge-way which the A354 has to climb between Dorchester and Weymouth. From the road, itself above a small tunnel, can be seen the south portal in local stone flanked by a massive cutting.

BOURNE VALLEY VIADUCTS, BRANKSOME
[SZ 062922] 112

Two elegant viaducts converge above Surrey Road as they cross the Bourne Valley. For brick, they are particularly fine, with decorated details and the use of some Portland stone. The Gas-works Curve or east viaduct became disused in 1967, but its partner carries the main LSWR line from Bournemouth to Poole. There are massive embankments too, made with material excavated by steam navvy from the long cutting to the east.

Bourne Valley viaducts.

CORFE CASTLE VIADUCT
[SY 960825] 113

A small viaduct overshadowed by the romantic ruins of Corfe Castle. It has four arches, in Purbeck stone, with a fancy date stone (1885) on the south side. Just to the north-west, a lane to Middlebere

Heath crosses twin stone bridges over the parallel courses of this Swanage branch line and the Fayle's narrow gauge tramway.

FRAMPTON TUNNEL
[SY 631951] 114

A good example of a cut-and-cover tunnel, constructed to preserve the lord of the manor's hunting rights. There is very little ground above a wide, round arch for twin broad gauge GWR tracks. The bridge over the now single line just north of Frampton village gives an excellent view of the long cutting and tunnel at the end.

GILLINGHAM STATION & BRIDGE
[ST 810261] 115

A small period station of the Salisbury and Exeter Railway (LSWR), with a lengthened platform on the 'up' side to Waterloo for the storage of milk churns destined for London. Opposite the station entrance is the old South Western Commercial Hotel and Posting House, built at the turn of the century. Gillingham was a busy place, for there were sidings to the Oake-Woods bacon factory (site 8), and the Gillingham brick and tile works which closed in 1968 to become an industrial estate.

Just east of the station is an iron road bridge over the line [ST 813262]. Strengthening steel girders were built above it in 1951, so that the B3081 to Shaftesbury crosses an exaggerated humped back, but the iron spans can be seen below, with a plate cast 'BRYMBO 1858'.

An ornate barrow and silver spade used to cut the first sod when building the railway are now displayed in the museum at Gillingham.

GRIMSTONE VIADUCT
[SY 640945] 116

A short but substantial stone bridge carries the GWR line over Sydling Water and a lane to Sydling St Nicholas. The centre arch is the largest of three and its piers each have four arched openings.

Grimstone viaduct.

MAIDEN NEWTON STATION
[SY 599980]　　　　　　117

A good example of a country station at a junction (GWR). Buildings on both platforms are well built of flint with Ham stone dressings and slate roofs. The disused bay for the Bridport branch remains. Just north, the grassed over cutting of that branch curves away under an iron road bridge. A brick signal box completes the scene.

POUNDBURY TUNNEL
[SY 682912]　　　　　　118

This tunnel takes the GWR line beneath Poundbury hillfort on the approach to Dorchester, an early example of the preservation of an archaeological monument (NB also the LSWR line was made to avoid Maumbury Rings at Dorchester). At the north end, the trace of the Roman aqueduct into Durnovaria can be seen on the slope just below the railway.

SANDLEY TUNNEL
[ST 775247]　　　　　　119

Adverse geological conditions caused many engineering difficulties when this tunnel was built in 1859. It can be seen from a lane overbridge to the east, while a lane above the west portal gives a fine view of the LSWR track (now single) across the vale to Templecombe in Somerset.

SHILLINGSTONE STATION
[ST 824117]　　　　　　120

The brick built station building survives with an unusually large canopy which has been attributed to Edward VII alighting here on visits to nearby Iwerne Minster House. Both platforms remain too. The Somerset & Dorset Railway Trust is preserving this lone survivor on this stretch of the line.

Shillingstone Station.

SWANAGE RAILWAY & STATION
[SZ 029789]　　　　　　12■

The Swanage Railway is now being relaid from Swanage, the intention being to restore a steam passenger service as far as Wareham. The station terminus has been restored and the yard is full of rolling stock. This is the centre of the project and has all the atmosphere of its earlier days. ☎ 092■ 425800.

WAREHAM STATION
[SY 920881]　　　　　　12:

A handsome Victorian station building, in brick with stone dressings, the LSWR's coat of arms and 1886 date stone. Decorated cast iron posts support the canopies on both platforms. The earlier station was just to the east where a brick engine shed survives.

Wareham Station.

WEST BAY STATION
[SY 465904]　　　　　　12

An attractive little station building with tall chimneys and the platform survive, but in a poor condition. West Bay was once busy with summer visitors, but not enough for this part of the Brid port line was closed to passengers in 1930.

WEYMOUTH TRAMWAY
[SY 680787]　　　　　　12

In 1865, a tramway was laid from Weymouth station along the quay to serve the cross channel steamers. Until the closing of the ferry service visitors to Weymouth had the extraordinary experience of witnessing trains sharing the road with motor cars.

PORTS & SHIPPING

ANVIL POINT LIGHTHOUSE
[SZ 029769]   125

This low lighthouse with attached keepers' accommodation was built in 1881. It is surrounded by the Durlston Head Country Park near Swanage.

KIMMERIDGE
[SY 909788]   126

Here are various ruins of piers associated with attempts to work shale. A quay and alum works were built in 1570, but most evidence is from the nineteenth century. A ruined pier of large stones, with sloping sides, was built by Wanostrocht & Co. in 1860, shortly after gaining a contract to produce gas from the Kimmeridge shale to light the streets of Paris. In 1883, the Kimmeridge Oil & Carbon Co. built a wooden pier a little to the north, and it can be seen where this projected from a stone sea wall. There is a display panel explaining the history of the site.

LULWORTH COVE
[SY 824799]   127

Cosens' pleasure steamers from Weymouth were once regular callers at this special cove well into the present century. The ruins of a much earlier curved stone pier are visible at low tide on the west side, and part of a limekiln was exposed in the cliff near the slipway until it was washed away in recent years. In the hamlet is a row of former coastguard cottages.

LYME REGIS
[SY 339915]   128

The Cobb is a famous and massive curving construction which acts as a breakwater to the harbour. Begun in the thirteenth century, it has been enlarged and repaired over the centuries and is finished in Portland stone.

POOLE QUAY
[SZ 009903]   129

Poole is still a busy port, although the Quay is used mainly by pleasure craft. Old warehouses are recognisable above tourist establishments. Between the Custom House, rebuilt after a fire in 1813, and the harbour office of 1822, is a fifteenth century woolhouse known as the Town Cellars. This stone building now contains the Maritime Museum which tells of Poole's seafaring past. Poole Bridge lifts to allow ships and other craft through to the inner harbour. It connects Poole with Hamworthy and was completed in 1927.

PORTLAND BILL LIGHTHOUSES
[SY 677684]   130

The impressive lighthouse of 1906 is 136' (41·4m) high, and the main light is visible for 18 miles (29 km). It is well worth visiting as the fog signal air compressors are also of interest. A plaque over the ground floor door is dated 1789, and came from the earlier lower lighthouse of 1789. The obelisk day-mark on the Bill in front of the lighthouse is inscribed 'T.H. 1844', referring to Trinity House (not Thomas Hardy!). The modern lighthouse replaced the Higher and Lower Lighthouses [SY 677693 & SY 681690], which were coal-fired when first built in 1716. The Lower Light was rebuilt in 1789 and was the first in the world to use a true lens. At the same time the Higher Light was the first in the country to be fitted with Argand oil lamps. The lighthouses seen today were built in 1869, and the lower one is now a bird observatory.

Portland Bill lighthouse.

PORTLAND BREAKWATER
[SY 706750]   131

A massive undertaking which was responsible for bringing the convict prison to Portland. The first breakwater was built under the direction of John Coode in 1849-72, and used 5¾ million tons of Portland stone, mostly hewn by convicts and brought to the site by the Breakwater Railway incline. Two new arms of the breakwater were added in 1895-1903, which gave the anchorage greater protection from torpedo attacks. The Portland naval base continues to thrive within the shelter of this great harbour.

ST ALDHELM'S HEAD
[SY 960757]   132

A row of nineteenth century coastguard cottages stands on this windswept and upstanding headland. There is a lookout on the edge of the cliff.

SWANAGE
[SZ 035787]   **133**

Swanage was a stone shipping port before it became a resort. There were stone bankers along the eighteenth century quay, and their products were carried into the water on large wheeled carts until they could be transferred to small barges. These took the stone out to larger vessels anchored in the bay. This inefficient system was replaced by a pier in 1859 when a tramway was laid from the bankers. The trade had declined by 1896 when a second pier was built. This was used by pleasure steamers, but both piers are now derelict.

WEST BAY
[SY 462904]   **134**

In the fourteenth century, attempts to make a harbour for Bridport at the mouth of the Brit soon became choked with sand and gravel. A harbour with sluices and piers was built in the 1740s, and much developed in 1823-5. Imports of hemp for ropemaking declined with the fortunes of that industry by the 1870s. With the opening of the railway, attempts were made to develop West Bay as a resort. Timber and coal continued to be brought in, while gravel from the beach was exported, but West Bay is now a fishing port. The dock walls are of tough Portland roach, approached through a narrow entrance between two piers. A dam holds back the River Brit and sluices allow the harbour to be scoured at low tide. A prominent three-storeyed warehouse in George Street has been converted to offices. It is hard to believe that wooden ships were built on the west side of the harbour in 1779-1885.

Weymouth Fishmarket ice house.

WEYMOUTH
[SY 680787]   **135**

Warehouses along Custom House Quay have been converted to restaurants and other tourist attractions. The Custom House is a former mer-

chant's house. Of special interest is the grey ston Fish Market and Ice House of 1855, with a wid canopied roof. The railway, which added a tram way along the quay to the pier in 1859, assure Weymouth's future as a ferry port with crossing to Cherbourg and the Channel Islands. Howeve services were withdrawn in the 1980s.

WHITEHEAD TORPEDO FACTORY, WYKE REGIS
[SY 667763]   **136**

Wellworthy Engineering now occupies part of the Whitehead Torpedo Factory, established by Robert Whitehead in 1891 near Ferrybridge, at Wyke Regis. This was on the edge of Portland harbour where it was closely associated with nava activities. A long pier was built into the water as part of a test range. The factory was modernised in 1934 and closed after the Second World War Whitehead had houses built nearby for his workers.

PUBLIC UTILITIES

BEAMINSTER GAS HOUSE
[ST 479001]   **13**

The Gas House is at the end of St Mary Well Lane and dates from 1839, just five years after the industry came here. Now a private house, i cream stone with brick details, its name is the onl clue to its origins.

BRIDPORT GAS WORKS
[SY 465923]   **13**

Bridport had the first gas works in the county when the Bridport Gas Co was established i 1831, and was the first in the county. Gas makin ceased in 1958 and most of the site has bee cleared. However, there are are two good ston buildings separated by the former gas works en trance in South Street. The manager's house has datestone 'BGC 1872' and is now a fish and chi shop, while the former showroom (1899) is motor cycle centre.

BRIDPORT POWER STATION
[SY 463933]   **13**

The Municipal Electric Power Station was opene in 1929. It was built by George Abbot & Son and a distinctive brick building with clerestory roof. It in St Swithins Road, Allington, and is still occupie by the South Western Electricity Board.

ridport Gas Works showroom.

CASTLETON PUMPING STATION, SHERBORNE
[ST 646169]   140

A small square building near the railway line at Castleton contains a large waterwheel, 26′ × 3′ 9″ (7·9m × 1·1m), made by Edward White of Redditch. It formerly obtained its water from a stream nd Sherborne Lake, and was installed in 1898 to replace an earlier wheel driving three vertical ram umps supplied in 1869 by Stothert & Pitt of Bath. These were in use until about 1960 but have since een scrapped. The wheel has been restored by ne Castleton Waterwheel Restoration Society, nd is open to the public on some summer Sundays.

ORCHESTER GAS WORKS
[Y 905695]   141

ome of the gas works buildings survive at this site w occupied by Wood's removal stores. A nice etail is the curving roadway off Icen Way, with one setts and two lines of granite slabs to bear e heavy wheels of traffic such as coal and coke hicles.

HAFTESBURY GAS WORK OTTAGES
[T 859229]   142

ne Shaftesbury Gas & Coke Co Ltd was established in 1836 to supply street lighting in the town. ne gas works site is now occupied by the ambunce station at Bimport, but alongside there reains an attractive a terrace of workers' cottages hich were built by the company.

SUTTON POYNTZ WATERWORKS
[SY 706839]   143

The Weymouth Water Co's works and pumping station, well constructed in limestone, with workers' cottages alongside. The Springhead water source is under the chalk escarpment, where the funnel of *Great Eastern* still serves as part of the reservoir overflow for 9m gallons per day. The water company bought the top 30′ (9·1m) of the funnel when the ship put into Portland Harbour after a boiler explosion on her maiden voyage in 1859. In the village, the sign of the Springhead Hotel depicts the funnel being drawn by horses to the waterworks.

WALFORD WATER WORKS, WIMBORNE
[SU 007009]   144

The distinctive works buildings, built in 1896-1904 with stylish brickwork and half-round roofs, can be viewed from a public footpath alongside. This was the first attempt by the Bournemouth Gas & Water Co. (now Bournemouth & District Water Co) to obtain pure water from deep underground, to supply the growing demands of Bournemouth. Steam pumping was by Simpson compound tandem engines, replaced in 1959 by electric pumps. Treatment plant was installed to soften the water and remove mineral deposits.

WEDGWOOD ELECTRICAL COLLECTION, CHRISTCHURCH
[SZ 156901]   145

Over 500 exhibits are housed in the engine and battery rooms of the former power station at Bargates, Christchurch. They explain over a century of development of the electricity supply industry. There are replicas of early laboratory equipment, generators, switchgear, transformers, appliances, lighting and wiring systems. A large generating set includes a Bellis & Morcom steam engine. Access is through the Curator, Southern Electricity, 25 Bourne Valley Road, Branksome, Poole. ☎ 0202 762828.

WEYMOUTH GAS TUNNEL
[SY 676789]   146

Except for the gasholder, the gas works in Westway Road has gone, but a stone feature in the Backwater contains a shaft which gave access to a tunnel carrying the gas main under the harbour to the town. Other stone structures further north were related to a dam to hold back Radipole lake.

FURTHER READING

Addison, J. & Wailes, R.   Dorset Watermills, *Trans. Newcomen Society*, XXXV (1962-3), 193-216.

Algar, D., Light, A. &
Copland-Griffiths, P.   The Verwood and District Potteries: A Dorset Industry (Verwood, 2nd ed. 1987)

Benfield, E.   Purbeck Shop: a Stoneworker's Story of Stone, (1940)

Bettey, J.   The Island and Royal Manor of Portland (1970)

Bone, M.   The Bridport Flax and Hemp Industry, *Bristol IA Soc. Journal*, 18 (1986), 19-31.

Chubb, L., et al,   Dorset Toll-House Survey (Dorset C C, 1977)

Cockburn, E.O.   The Stone Quarries of Dorset (DNHAS Mansel-Pleydell Prize Essay, 1971)

Davies, W.K.J.   Pike Bros, Fayle & Co. Ltd., Furzebrook (Narrow-gauge Railway Society, 1957)

Dewar, H.S.L.   The Windmills, Watermills and Horsemills of Dorset, *Proceedings of Dorset Nat Hist & Arch Soc*, vol 82 (1960), 109-132.

Good, R.   The Old Roads of Dorset (new edition, 1966)

Gow, W.G., et al,   Dorset Milestone Survey (Dorset C C, 1980)

Leach, R.   An Investigation into the use of Purbeck Marble in Medieval England (Crediton, 2nd ed, 1978)

Legg, R.   Purbeck Island (Wincanton, revised edition, 1989)
Purbeck's Heath (1987)

Lucking, J.H.   Dorset Railways (Wimborne, 1982)

Morris, S.   Portland: an illustrated history (Wimborne, 1985)

Sanctuary, A.   Rope, Twine and Net Making (Shire, 2nd ed. 1988)

Saville, R.J.   The Industrial Archaeology and Transport of Purbeck (Globe Education, 1976)
Langton's Stone Quarries (Langton Matravers, 2nd ed 1986)

Seekings, J.   Thomas Hardy's Brewer: the story of Eldridge Pope & Co (Wimborne, 1988)

Stevenson, W.   A General View of the Agriculture of Dorsetshire (1812)

Wallis, A.J.   Dorset Bridges, A History & Guide (Abbey Press, 1974)

Wear, R. & Lees, E.   Stephen Lewin & the Poole Foundry (1978)

Young, D.   Brickmaking in Dorset, *Proceedings of Dorset Nat Hist & Arch Soc*, vol 93 (1971), 213-242.

Young, J.   Old Dorset Brewers (1986)

SOCIETIES

Dorset Industrial Archaeology Society
Brenda Innes, 10 Gold Hill, Shaftesbury, SP7 8HB

Castleton Waterwheel Restoration Society
Graham Bendall, 2 St Mary's Road, Sherborne, DT9 6DG

Poole Industrial Archaeology Group
Bill Hines, 22 Sark Road, Parkstone, Poole, BH12 3PN

Verwood & District Potteries Trust
Secretary, 10 Bridport Road, Verwood

ACKNOWLEDGEMENTS

Special thanks are given to Mike Bone for assis tance with the breweries and Bridport industries Also to Alan Bailey, Graham Bendall, Penny Co pland-Griffiths, Martin Hammond, Leslie Hayward Bill Hines, Tony and Brenda Innes, Jude James Michael Lester, Brian Miller, Roger Peers, Rolan Tarr, Brian Toop, Derrick Warren, Tony Yowar and all others who have helped in small ways.

Front cover: Waterwheel at Old Brewery, Bridport.